NATIONAL GEOGRAPHIC LEARNING | CENGAGE Learning

T0346294

GRAMMAR BOOSTER 3

Rachel Finnie

Megan Roderick

Grammar Booster 3
Rachel Finnie, Megan Roderick

Acknowledgements
Illustrated by Panagiotis Angeletakis

ISBN: 978-960-403-101-6 Student's Book

ISBN: 978-960-403-102-3 Teacher's Book

National Geographic Learning
Cheriton House, North Way, Andover, Hampshire, SP10 5BE
United Kingdom

Cengage Learning is a leading provider of customized learning solutions with office locations around the globe, including Singapore, the United Kingdom, Australia, Mexico, Brazil and Japan. Locate your local office at:
international.cengage.com/region

Cengage Learning products are represented in Canada by Nelson Education, Ltd.

Visit National Geographic Learning online at **ngl.cengage.com**

Visit our corporate website at **www.cengage.com**

Printed in the United Kingdom by Lightning Source
Print Number: 08   Print Year: 2017

Contents

Present Simple & Present Continuous

Present Simple

Affirmative	**Negative**	**Question**
I/you read	I/you do not (don't) read	Do I/you read?
he/she/it reads	he/she/it does not (doesn't) read	Does he/she/it read?
we/you/they read	we/you/they do not (don't) read	Do we/you/they read?

Short answers

Yes, I/you do.	No, I/you don't.
Yes, he/she/it does.	No, he/she/it doesn't.
Yes, we/you/they do.	No, we/you/they don't.

We use the Present Simple to talk about:

- habits.
  She sees her grandmother every weekend.
  He doesn't go skiing twice a week.

- things that are true in general.
  The sun sets in the west.
  It is often cold in winter.

- permanent states.
  We live in Paris.
  She works as a secretary.

Notes
We can use negative questions when we want to show that we are surprised about something.
Aren't you ready yet?

1 Complete the sentences with the Present Simple.

Eg   I ....*go*.......... to the gym every week. (go)

1   She .... all her money on clothes. (spend)

2   They .... meat. (not eat)

3   It .... cold and wet in winter. (be)

4   My teacher .... from Ireland. (come)

5   We .... them very often. (not see)

6   The headmaster .... in his office all day long. (sit)

7   My sister only .... TV on Saturdays. (watch)

8   Water .... at zero degrees Celsius. (freeze)

9   He .... golf at the weekend. (play)

10   I .... German. (not speak)

2 Complete the questions with the Present Simple.

Eg   ..*Does she*.. always ....*complain*.... so much? (she / complain)

1   .... ever .... any work? (he / do)

2   .... in France? (they / live)

3   .... any milk? (we / need)

4   .... the way to the restaurant? (they / know)

5   .... usually .... the housework? (you / do)

6   .... him with his work? (his wife / help)

7   .... very hot in the summer? (the weather / get)

8   .... out with his friends every day? (he / go)

9   .... in the school choir? (she / sing)

10   .... abroad every summer? (you / travel)

Adverbs of Frequency with the Present Simple

never	rarely	sometimes	often	usually	always
0%					100%

Adverbs of frequency come before the main verb but after the verb *to be*.
He often watches TV in the evening.
She is often late for school.

5

Rewrite the sentences with the adverbs of frequency in the correct place.

Eg *She goes swimming in the winter. (never)*
    She never goes swimming in the winter.

1   They have time to relax. (rarely)

    ....

2   We meet her at the café. (sometimes)

    ....

3   Are they at home in the evenings? (always)

    ....

4   Does the train leave on time? (usually)

    ....

5   It is very cold here in winter. (rarely)

    ....

6   Dad plays cards with Mum. (sometimes)

    ....

7   Do you have a lot of homework? (often)

    ....

8   She is on time for her appointments. (never)

    ....

Time Expressions with the Present Simple

every day	in the mornings
every week	in the afternoons
every month	in the evenings
every year	on Mondays
every summer	on Wednesday mornings
every other day	three times a day
every two months	once a week
at the weekend	twice a month
in December	

Time Expressions usually come at the end of a sentence. We put them at the beginning of a sentence when we want to emphasise them.
He pays his telephone bill every two months.
On Saturday mornings we clean the house.

4 Write sentences which are true about yourself using the time expressions given.

Eg (every summer) *I go on a beach holiday every summer.*

1   (at the weekend) ....

2   (in the evenings) ....

3   (every week) ....

4   (once a month) ....

5   (twice a day) ....

6   (in December) ....

7   (every year) ....

8   (on Saturdays) ....

Present Continuous

Affirmative	Negative	Question
I am (I'm) reading	I am not (I'm not) reading	Am I reading?
you are (you're) reading	you are not (aren't) reading	Are you reading?
he/she/it is (he's/she's/it's) reading	he/she/it is not (isn't) reading	Is he/she/it reading?
we/you/they are (we're/you're/they're) reading	we/you/they are not (aren't) reading	Are we/you/they reading?

Short answers

Yes, I am.	No, I'm not.
Yes, you are.	No, you aren't.
Yes, he/she/it is.	No, he/she/it isn't.
Yes, we/you/they are.	No, we/you/they aren't.

We use the Present Continuous to talk about:

- actions in progress at the time of speaking.
  She is making lunch now.
  Is he using the computer at the moment?

- actions in progress around the time of speaking.
  We're staying with my grandparents this week.
  They are learning Russian this year.

Notes
We can use negative questions when we want to show that we are surprised about something.
Why aren't you eating your lunch?

---

5 Complete the sentences with the words from the box. Use the Present Continuous.

catch	celebrate	go	listen	make	repair
stay	talk	teach	watch	work	

Eg *The workmen* ...*are repairing*... *the hole in the road.*

1 I .... the bus to work this morning.

2 He (not) .... long in Canada.

3 I think I .... to the wrong person.

4 She (not) .... to school today.

5 We .... the fireworks display. Isn't it wonderful?

6 I .... a cake for my son's birthday.

7 My grandparents .... their golden wedding anniversary today.

8 They (not) .... to what he is telling them.

9 Maria .... her dog to do tricks.

10 The washing machine (not) .... – I'll have to wash the clothes by hand.

6 Complete the questions with the Present Continuous.

Eg ......*Is the baby sleeping*...... at the moment? *(the baby / sleep)*

1   What ....? *(you / eat)*
2   .... all the way across Europe? *(they / drive)*
3   .... something nice? *(she / cook)*
4   .... for clothes? *(you / shop)*
5   Why .... his homework? *(he / not do)*
6   .... on the computer? *(Dad / work)*
7   .... pizza for dinner? *(they / order)*
8   .... money for the poor? *(the students / collect)*
9   .... a meeting for Saturday? *(he / organise)*
10 .... all their friends? *(they / invite)*

THINK ABOUT IT!

*Questions in the Present Simple or the Present Continuous have the same word order when they start with question words (**what, why,** etc).*

Time Expressions with the Present Continuous

at the moment
for the time being
now
right now
this morning
this afternoon
this week
this month
this year
today

7 Complete the sentences with the Present Simple or Present Continuous.

Eg   We usually ......*have*...... lunch at one o'clock. *(have)*

1   When I .... on holiday in the summer, I .... in the sea every day. *(go, swim)*
2   The children .... to music in their bedroom at the moment. *(listen)*
3   What .... on Saturdays? *(you / do)*
4   They .... in a rented flat for the time being because the builders .... on their new house. *(live, work)*
5   We .... ready to go out just now, so I can't spend long on the phone. *(get)*
6   What .... usually .... for breakfast? *(you / have)*
7   What language ....? Is it Spanish? *(those tourists / speak)*
8   She rarely .... television because she .... to read a good book. *(watch, prefer)*

8

Stative Verbs

We don't usually use stative verbs in the Present Continuous. Stative verbs are:

- **verbs of senses.**
  feel, hear, see, smell, sound, taste
  The soup tastes delicious!

- **verbs of feeling.**
  dislike, hate, like, love, need, prefer, want
  He doesn't like talking in public.

- **verbs of understanding.**
  appear, believe, forget, hope, imagine, know,
  mean, remember, seem, think, understand
  She seems to be unhappy about something.

- **verbs of possession.**
  belong to, own
  That car belongs to my sister.

We can use some stative verbs in the Present Continuous, but there is a change in meaning.

When we use the verb *see* in the Present Continuous it means *meet* or *visit*.
I'm seeing my friends tomorrow.

The verb *think* usually means *have the opinion* or *believe*.
I think his new car is wonderful.

When we use the verb *think* in the Present Continuous, it means *use the mind*.
Please be quiet! I'm thinking.

Notes
We often use the verbs of senses with the verb *can*.
I can hear the telephone.
My father can't see very well without his glasses.

8 Choose the correct answer.

Eg   *I am needing / need a haircut.*

1   *Do you think / Are you thinking* that his latest record is his best?
2   Granny *is forgetting / forgets* all our birthdays!
3   Paul *is understanding / understands* the problem.
4   What *do you think / are you thinking* about?
5   *I hope / I'm hoping to* I see you soon.
6   He *doesn't remember / isn't remembering* her name.
7   *Is this bag belonging / Does this bag belong* to you?
8   They *don't seem / aren't seeming* to be there.
9   Yes, I *see / am seeing* what you mean.
10   I can't go with you to the cinema tomorrow; I *see / am seeing* Jackie.

Complete the radio report with the Present Simple or Present Continuous.

Good day to all our listeners!

I (Eg) .... *am sitting* .... (sit) here in the heat, watching a herd of elephants nearby. They
(1) .... (have) a nice bath in the river! About twenty elephants are here in
all, including some very young ones. I (2) .... (hide) in some long grass away
from the elephants, so they (3) .... (not see) me.
You (4) .... (not usually find) elephants playing like this but the young ones
(5) .... (love) the water and they also (6) ....
(enjoy) shooting water at their friends with their trunks! I certainly (7) ....
(think) the elephants (8) .... (have) a nice time – I would like to have a
swim too! I (9) .... (stay) in Zanzibar for a few days so I
(10) .... (hope) to report on more interesting wild animals very soon!

Goodbye for now from Zanzibar!

Read the e-mail and correct the tenses.

Internet Explorer

Back   Forward   Stop   Refresh   Home   AutoFill   Print   Mail
Address:

Dear George,
How are you? I'm very well. At the moment (Eg) *I send* .... *I'm sending* .... you an e-mail because
I (1) <u>am wanting</u> .... to know your latest news. (2) <u>Do you have</u>
.... a nice time at the moment? What subjects (3) <u>are you liking</u>
.... at school? I (4) <u>am going</u> .... to the gym three
times a week and I (5) <u>learn</u> .... to play the guitar this year. School is OK but I
(6) <u>am preferring</u> .... the weekends! My sister (7) <u>studies</u> ....
at university this year so she is very busy.

I (8) <u>am hoping</u> .... to hear from you soon.

All the best,
Tom

100%   Doc: 653K/525K

11 Choose the correct answer.

Eg Ian .... on his computer at the moment.
 a works   **b** is working   **c** work

1 What time .... you go to work in the mornings?
 a does   **b** do   **c** are

2 .... she speaking to her best friend on the phone?
 a Is   **b** Does   **c** Do

3 I feel worried because I .... about all my problems!
 a am thinking   **b** think   **c** think to

4 He .... on the computer every day.
 a work   **b** is working   **c** works

5 We .... English lessons every other day.
 a are having   **b** have   **c** having

6 They .... all their friends to the party.
 a don't invite   **b** don't inviting   **c** aren't inviting

7 She .... watching horror films.
 a doesn't like   **b** isn't liking   **c** likes not

8 .... you help your parents with the housework?
 a Are   **b** Is   **c** Do

Pairwork

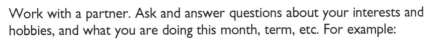

Work with a partner. Ask and answer questions about your interests and hobbies, and what you are doing this month, term, etc. For example:

- What do you do in your free time?
- How often do you play football?
- Are you learning a foreign language this year?
- Are you singing in the school choir this term?

Writing

Send an e-mail to a friend, telling him/her what you are doing this year. Talk about your hobbies, your studies and what the other members of your family are doing.

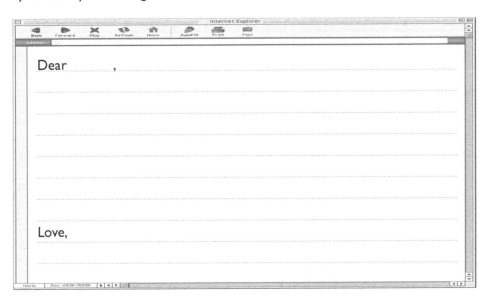

Dear   ,

Love,

Past Simple, Past Continuous & Used To

Past Simple – Regular Verbs

Affirmative	Negative	Question
I/you started	I/you did not (didn't) start	Did I/you start?
he/she/it started	he/she/it did not (didn't) start	Did he/she/it start?
we/you/they started	we/you/they did not (didn't) start	Did we/you/they start?

Short answers	
Yes, I/you did.	No, I/you didn't.
Yes, he/she/it did.	No, he/she/it didn't.
Yes, we/you/they did.	No, we/you/they didn't.

Past Simple – Irregular Verbs

Affirmative	Negative	Question
I/you ate	I/you did not (didn't) eat	Did I/you eat?
he/she/it ate	he/she/it did not (didn't) eat	Did he/she/it eat?
we/you/they ate	we/you/they did not (didn't) eat	Did we/you/they eat?

Short answers	
Yes, I/you did.	No, I/you didn't.
Yes, he/she/it did.	No, he/she/it didn't.
Yes, we/you/they did.	No, we/you/it didn't.

We use the Past Simple to talk about:

- actions that started and finished in the past.
  She washed the dishes last night.
  Did you go to America last summer?

- actions that happened one after the other in the past.
  He opened the fridge, took out the bread and ham and made a sandwich.

- actions that were repeated or were habits in the past.
  My mother walked to work every day.
  People rode horses then.

See the Irregular Verbs list on page 168.

1 Complete the sentences with the Past Simple.

Eg They .... *didn't go* .... to the cinema. (not go)
1 .... all the food from the supermarket? (you / buy)
2 I .... the letters to America. (send)
3 .... about the meeting? (he / know)
4 We .... a lot of people to help us. (need)
5 .... on time? (the concert / start)
6 My friend .... last night. (not phone)
7 They .... a great time at the party. (have)
8 I .... to work yesterday. (not drive)

2 Match the questions and the answers.

Eg *Where did you go last night?*   a Peter did.
1 Who won the prize?   b No, they didn't.
2 How did you know?   c It was quite good.
3 What did you think of it?   d Down the road on the left.
4 Why didn't they come tonight?   e Because I was there.
5 Didn't they say they were sorry?   f This afternoon.
6 Did she decide to change her job?   g I think they were too tired.
7 Where is the nearest supermarket?   h I don't think so.
8 When did you arrive?   i *Out for a meal.*

Time Expressions with the Past Simple

a week ago   last summer
a month ago   last year
a year ago   on Saturday
in January   on 29th August, etc
in 1995   the day before yesterday
in my youth   the other day
last night   when I was five years old
last week   yesterday

Time expressions come at the beginning or the end of a sentence.

13

Write sentences using the Past Simple.

Eg   *a horse / ride / in the summer holidays / I*
     I rode a horse in the summer holidays.
     ....

I   have / we / last Saturday / a great party
     ....

2   on a skiing holiday / David and Judy / in February / go
     ....

3   seven years old / not learn / to swim / I be / when / I
     ....

4   leave / yesterday / Angela
     ....

5   buy / two years / they / ago / the house
     ....

6   *Friends* / last night / watch / you / ?
     ....

7   the other day / see / a fox / we
     ....

8   buy / the day before yesterday / the children / some books
     ....

Past Continuous

Affirmative	Negative	Question
I was working	I was not (wasn't) working	Was I working?
you were working	you were not (weren't) working	Were you working?
he/she/it was working	he/she/it was not (wasn't) working	Was he/she/it working?
we/you/they were working	we/you/they were not (weren't) working	Were we/you/they working?

Short answers

Yes, I was.	No, I wasn't.
Yes, you were.	No, you weren't.
Yes, he/she/it was.	No, he/she/it wasn't.
Yes, we/you/they were.	No, we/you/they weren't.

We use the Past Continuous to talk about:

- actions that were in progress at a specific time in the past.
  I was watching TV at nine o'clock yesterday.
  She wasn't working when I saw her.

- two or more actions that were in progress at the same time in the past.
  Mum was making lunch and I was doing my homework.
  My brother was playing a game and I was watching him.

- the background events in a story.
  It was snowing and the wind was blowing.
  The sun was shining and the birds were singing.

- an action in progress in the past that was interrupted by another.
  I was washing the car when it started to rain.
  She was having a bath when the phone rang.

Time Expressions with the Past Continuous

all day yesterday	last Sunday
all evening	last year
at ten o'clock last night	this morning

4 Complete the sentences with the Past Continuous.

Eg She ....*was talking*....... on the phone for most of the evening. *(talk)*

1 He wasn't at home yesterday because he .... an exam. *(take)*

2 We .... the salad and Sam was laying the table. *(make)*

3 The builders .... hard for several weeks on the house. *(work)*

4 The baby .... when I went to see her. *(not cry)*

5 No one .... to the radio so we switched it off. *(listen)*

6 The students .... very hard because they were tired. *(not try)*

7 At eight o'clock on Saturday evening, they .... ready to go out. *(get)*

8 It .... very hard all day yesterday. *(rain)*

9 He .... his book, he was listening to his new CD! *(not read)*

10 Dad .... John how to use the Internet this morning. *(show)*

5 Complete the questions with the Past Continuous.

Eg What ....*were you looking for*....... in the cupboard? *(you / look for)*

1 .... in the garden all day yesterday? *(the children / play)*

2 .... the newspaper all evening? *(Dad / read)*

3 What .... on television? *(he / watch)*

4 Who .... on the door this morning? *(knock)*

5 .... all night long? *(it / rain)*

6 .... in Paris last year? *(they / live)*

7 Who .... to on the phone at eleven o'clock last night? *(you / talk)*

8 .... bread all morning? *(you / make)*

When and While

We use *when* with the Past Simple.
I was listening to the teacher when the fire alarm started to ring.
When I got home, my brother was listening to music.

We use *while* with the Past Continuous.
I arrived while the children were singing a song.
While I was doing the housework, my mother phoned.

6 Complete the sentences with **when** or **while**.

Eg *I was studying* ....*while*......... *I was listening to music.*

1 .... he called, I was just getting ready.
2 .... we were eating, we talked about her studies.
3 .... the door opened, the professor came in.
4 He was studying .... suddenly he fell asleep.
5 .... I was eating, I found a caterpillar in the salad!
6 He was mending the bike .... he was talking on his mobile phone.
7 Did you see anything interesting .... you were visiting Italy?
8 It was already late .... they got home.

THINK
ABOUT IT!

For an action in the past which only took a short time we use **when**.

7 Imagine you are Detective Whodunnit and you are investigating the murder of Mr X.
In front of you is one of the main suspects, Mr Strange. Complete the questions using the Past Simple or the Past Continuous to find out exactly where he was at the time of the murder.

Eg *Where* ....*were you*................. *on the night of 12th September? (be)*

1 What .... between the hours of 9 and 11 pm? (you / do)
2 Who .... with? (you / be)
3 What .... at the restaurant? (you / eat)
4 What ....? (you / drink)
5 .... the restaurant at any time during the evening? (you / leave)
6 .... Mr X very well? (you / know)
7 How often .... him? (you / see)
8 .... any arguments with him? (you / have)

8 Use Detective Whodunnit's notes and write Mr Strange's answers to the questions in exercise 7.

Suspect: Mr Strange

12th September?	Blue Sky Restaurant
Between 9 and 11?	meal at Blue Sky Restaurant
Who with?	with three friends
Food?	steak, chips, salad
Drink?	beer
Left restaurant?	9-10 pm to pick up another friend
Know Mr X?	good friends with him
How often see him?	3 or 4 times a year
Argument?	no arguments

Eg *I was at the Blue Sky Restaurant on the night of 12th September.*

1 ....
2 ....
3 ....
4 ....
5 ....
6 ....
7 ....
8 ....

Used To

Affirmative	Negative	Question
I/you used to play	I/you did not (didn't) use to play	Did I/you use to play?
he/she/it used to play	he/she/it did not (didn't) use to play	Did he/she/it use to play?
we/you/they used to play	we/you/they did not (didn't) use to play	Did we/you/they use to play?

Short answers

Yes, I/you did.	No, I/you didn't.
Yes, he/she/it did.	No, he/she/it didn't.
Yes, we/you/they did.	No, we/you/they didn't.

We use *used to* for actions that we did regularly in the past but that we don't do now. We also use it for states that existed in the past but that don't exist now.
I used to play football every Saturday morning, but now I don't have time.
We used to live in Brighton, but now we live in Sevenoaks.

Notes
We can use the Past Simple and *used to* for past habits and states that don't happen now. There is no change in meaning, but we must use a time expression with the Past Simple.
She used to work in the city.
She worked in the city two years ago.

9 Complete the sentences with the correct form of **used to** and the verb in brackets.

Eg *He .... didn't use to like .... studying but he does now. (not like)*

1 I .... my mother in the house when I had more time. (help)

2 .... around the corner from the school? (you / live)

3 .... a dog? (they / have)

4 I .... to bed late when I was a child. (not go)

5 .... a lot of television? (you / watch)

6 She .... two houses but she sold them last year. (own)

7 We .... a lot but now we eat out about once a week. (not eat out)

8 They .... for walks on Sundays. (go)

9 .... a lot of letters? (you / write)

10 I .... the piano well when I was a child. (play)

Rewrite the sentences using the words given. Use between two and five words.

Eg	*They had a little house by the sea when they lived in Spain.* **used**
	They .... used to have .... a little house by the sea.

1	During lunch, someone knocked at the door. **having**
	While we ...., someone knocked at the door.

2	Was your last car a Fiat? **use**
	Did .... a Fiat before this car?

3	They watched a lot of cartoons when they were young. **used**
	They .... a lot of cartoons.

4	I could hear his CD player while he was working. **listening**
	He .... CD player while he was working.

5	We didn't like vegetables when we were young. **use**
	We .... vegetables.

Find the extra word in each line and write it in the space. Four of the lines are correct.

Eg	*One day, I was always walking along the road on my*	.... *always* ....

1	way to work. It was a lovely morning; the sun it was	....

2	shining and the birds were singing. I used felt quite	....

3	happy and everything was going well. I started to	....

4	think about the things did I used to do when I was young.	....

5	I did used to go to school on my bike and it was	....

6	always a good way to start the day! My friends used to	....

7	ride their bikes too, so we all went together. Once we	....

8	were found a young cat on the road and we took it to	....

9	the vet because it not had a broken leg. The vet thanked	....

10	us for looking after the poor animal! We had fun when	....

	we were young!

12 Read the story and correct the tenses.

All of us dream of finding some lost treasure. Well, one day last summer, I (Eg) _was reading_

...................._read_.................... an article in the newspaper about some treasure that was somewhere near

our village! I (1) _wasn't telling_ .... anyone about it but I (2) _was rushing_

.... out of the house with the newspaper in my hand and (3) _was going_

.... along a road that leads into the country. I (4) _was cycling_ ....

there a lot when I was a child and I (5) _was knowing_ .... the area very well. The

article said that the person who (6) _was wanting_ .... to find the treasure, should

dig under a very old tree. I (7) _was finding_ .... the tree in the middle of a field.

Now I (8) _was having_ .... to find the treasure!

Pairwork

In the story in Exercise 12, there aren't any descriptive sentences about the weather, the scenery, etc. Work together with your partner to write four descriptive sentences for the composition and decide where they should go.

1 ....

2 ....

3 ....

4 ....

Writing

Write a story about something strange that happened to you. Remember to include both the events that happened and a description of your feelings, the scenery, etc. Use the Past Simple and Past Continuous tenses.

A Strange Story

....

....

....

....

....

....

....

....

Present Perfect Simple & Present Perfect Continuous

Present Perfect Simple

Affirmative

I/you have (I've/you've) started
he/she/it has (he's/she's/it's) started
we/you/they have (we've/you've/they've) started

Negative

I/you have not (haven't) started
he/she/it has not (hasn't) started
we/you/they have not (haven't) started

Question

Have I/you started?
Has he/she/it started?
Have we/you/they started?

Short answers

Yes, I/you have.　　No, I/you haven't.
Yes, he/she/it has.　No, he/she/it hasn't.
Yes, we/you/they have.　No, we/you/they haven't.

The Present Perfect Simple is formed with the verb *have/has* + past participle of the main verb.

We use the Present Perfect Simple to talk about:

■ something that happened in the past but we don't know when.
She has started a new job.
Have they moved into their new house?

■ something that happened in the past but is important now.
She has eaten Chinese food, so she knows what it is like.
I have seen that film, so I don't want to get it out on video.

■ something that started in the past but continues now.
We have lived in this house for six years.
He hasn't worked here for long.

■ something that has just happened.
It has just started to rain.
We have just come back from holiday.

■ experiences and achievements.
I have visited fourteen different countries.
She has passed her driving test.

See page 168 for the Irregular Verbs list.

1

Complete the sentences with the Present Perfect Simple.

Eg It ....*hasn't rained*................ a lot this year. (not / rain)

1 She .... England three times. (visit)

2 They .... all the books yet. (not read)

3 We .... lunch. (finish)

4 I .... three new CDs so far this week. (buy)

5 .... the same job for fifteen years? (he / have)

6 We .... three tests this month. (write)

7 He .... his presents yet. (not open)

8 .... to switch off the lights? (I / forget)

9 It .... quite hot this month. (be)

10 The teacher .... the lesson. (start)

Time Expressions with the Present Perfect Simple

already	three times
ever	since 1995
for	since Christmas
for a long time/for ages	since June
just	so far
never	until now
once	yet
twice	

2

Complete the sentences with the correct time expression from the box.

already   ever   for   just   never   since   so far   twice   yet

Eg You don't need to make lunch. I have ....*already*............ done it.

1 Have you .... seen an elephant?

2 We have done three units of this book .... this year.

3 I waited .... three hours and then I went home.

4 Cindy has .... travelled abroad but she wants to.

5 I have read this book .... It was brilliant!

6 They have .... come back from the beach and their hair is still wet.

7 Jane hasn't phoned me .... last week.

8 Haven't you finished doing your hair ....?

Complete the questions with the Present Perfect Simple and write answers.

Eg *Have you watered* the flowers today? ✓
Yes, I have.

1 .... Indian food?
(you ever / eat) ✗
....

2 .... his homework?
(he / finish) ✓
....

3 .... your supper yet?
(you / have) ✗
....

4 .... to bed?
(they / go) ✓
....

5 .... the cooker on?
(you / leave) ✓
....

6 .... the meeting for
Monday? (she / arrange) ✓
....

THINK ABOUT IT!

*We often use **ever** in questions with the Present Perfect Simple and **never** in negative sentences.*

7 .... the good news?
(you / hear) ✓
....

8 .... in a plane?
(she ever / fly) ✓
....

9 .... the new series on TV?
(you / see) ✗
....

10 .... enough food for the party?
(we / cook) ✓
....

Have Been and Have Gone

We use *have been* to say that someone has gone to a place and has come back or that they have had an experience.
He has been to that restaurant twice.
She has been skiing before.

We use *have gone* to say that someone has gone to a place and not returned yet.
Mum has gone to the bank.
They have gone to the supermarket.

Complete the sentences with **have / has been** or **have / has gone**.

Eg She *has gone* to the supermarket and will be back in half an hour.

1 I .... to Spain on holiday several times.
2 .... you ever .... to that cinema to see a film?
3 James .... to work and will be back later.
4 You don't need to go to the supermarket. I .... already ....
5 Where is everybody?
   They .... all ....
6 They .... never .... to London, but they would like to go.
7 I .... to the chemist's twice and it was closed both times.
8 I asked them to wait for me but they .... already ....

Present Perfect Continuous

Affirmative

I/you have (I've/you've) been playing
he/she/it has (he's/she's/it's) been playing
we/you/they have (we've/you've/they've) been playing

Negative

I/you have not (haven't) been playing
he/she/it has not (hasn't) been playing
we/you/they have not (haven't) been playing

Question

Have I/you been playing?
Has he/she/it been playing?
Have we/you/they been playing?

Short answers

Yes, I/you have.   No, I/you haven't.
Yes, he/she/it has.   No, he/she/it hasn't.
Yes, we/you/they have.   No, we/you/they haven't.

The Present Perfect Continuous is formed with the verb *have/has* + *been* + the main verb + *-ing*.

We use the Present Perfect Continuous to talk about:

- something that started in the past and has happened repeatedly or has continued until now.
  I have been telephoning you all morning.
  He has been playing the same record for ages!

- something that happened repeatedly in the past and that may have finished now, but has results that we can see now.
  (He looks tired.) *Mark has been working in the garden.*
  (Her hair is wet.) *Susan has been swimming.*

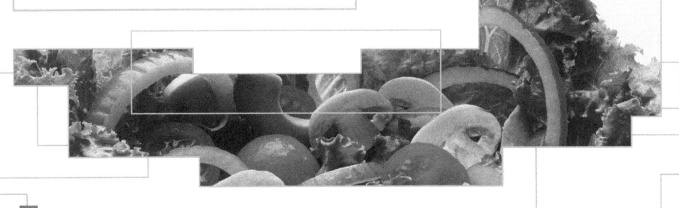

5 Complete the sentences with the Present Perfect Continuous.

Eg   I ...*have been working*... hard. *(work)*

1   She .... all morning. (cook)

2   They .... here for very long. (not live)

3   I'm so tired! I .... around all day! (rush)

4   We .... English for several years. (study)

5   .... properly? (she / eat)

6   Pete .... his homework for three hours! (do)

7   They .... around the town and they are exhausted! (walk)

8   .... your skiing holiday? (you / plan)

9   The children .... quietly in their bedroom all evening. (play)

10   I'm afraid I .... to what you were saying. (not listen)

Time Expressions with the Present Perfect Continuous

all day	for years
all night	lately
for a long time	recently
for (very) long	since

Notes

We use *for (very) long* in questions and negative sentences.
Have you been waiting for very long?

6 Write sentences with the Present Perfect Continuous.

Eg *You / work / too hard (lately)*
   You've been working too hard lately.
   ....

1   He / write / his book / two years (for)
   ....
   ....

2   I / not read / much (recently)
   ....
   ....

3   We / wait / here (for a long time)
   ....
   ....

4   They / prepare / for the party (all day)
   ....
   ....

5   I / play / the piano / I / be / four (since)
   ....
   ....

6   Sam / clean / the house / 10 am (since)
   ....
   ....

7 Complete the questions with the Present Perfect Continuous and write answers.

Eg   ...*Have you been cooking*... fish? (you / cook) ✓
     ...*Yes, I have.*...

1   .... hard this term?
    (the boys / study) ✗
    ....

2   .... late this week?
    (the post / arrive) ✓
    ....

3   .... a lot of headaches
    recently? (you / have) ✓
    ....

4   .... strangely recently?
    (he / behave) ✗
    ....

5   .... more milk than usual?
    (the baby / drink) ✓
    ....

6   .... football this afternoon?
    (you / play) ✗
    ....

7   .... a lot of things?
    (they / buy) ✓
    ....

8   .... to mend the iron?
    (he / try) ✓
    ....

9   .... too many sweets lately?
    (she / eat) ✓
    ....

10 .... easier?
    (the work / get) ✗
    ....

Present Perfect Simple or Present Perfect Continuous?

We use the Present Perfect Simple to talk about something we have done or achieved or an action that is complete.
I have finished all my work.
We have written twenty letters today.

We use the Present Perfect Continuous to talk about something that has lasted for a long time. It doesn't matter whether the action is complete or not.
They have been painting the kitchen all morning.
She has been studying all night.

8 Complete the sentences with the Present Perfect Simple or the Present Perfect Continuous.

Eg I ......*have eaten*...... three apples today. (eat)

1 They .... with the children all afternoon. (play)

2 She .... all her jobs for today. (finish)

3 I .... to lots of European countries. (travel)

4 We .... about the problem for days. (talk)

5 They .... all morning and they are exhausted! (shop)

6 Mike .... since 6 am and it's now 11 pm! (study)

7 Mum .... the ingredients. Shall we make the cake now?(buy)

8 He .... what car he wants to buy. (not decide)

9 .... all morning? (it / snow)

10 .... his book? He looks bored. (he / finish)

9 Look at the chart to see what the Roberts Family have been doing. Then write sentences using the Present Perfect Simple and the Present Perfect Continuous.

	What have they been doing?	What have they done?
Mum and Dad	do the washing-up	break three glasses
The boys	play football	break a window
Marie	listen to CDs	not do any homework
Biff the dog	dig for bones in the garden	make lots of holes
Granny	do the housework	not clean the whole house
Grandad	read the newspaper	read half the newspaper

Eg Mum and Dad *have been doing the washing-up. They have broken three glasses.*

1 The boys ....

2 Marie ....

3 Biff the dog ....

4 Granny ....

5 Grandad ....

25

10 Complete the dialogue with the Present Perfect Simple or the Present Perfect Continuous.

Mark: Hi, Tim. Where (Eg) ....*have you been*........... (be) all day? I (1) .... (look) for you!

Tim: Hello, Mark. Sorry, I (2) .... (be) out all day. The basketball team I play for (3) .... (train) for the big match on Saturday and I had to stay. What (4) .... (you / do), apart from looking for me?

Mark: Well, the girls and I (5) .... (walk) by the sea and we (6) .... (drink) coffee most of the day, while we were waiting for you! We (7) .... (not have) anything to eat yet, so shall we go for a pizza?

Helen: Come on, Tim. You (8) .... (run) around all day, so you must be starving! Let's go!

11 Choose the correct answer.

Eg I *have been working* / have worked *hard all day long.*

1 We *have invited / have been inviting* them to the party.

2 We *have chosen / have been choosing* new furniture all weekend.

3 *Have you been eating / Have you eaten* all your food?

4 I *have been reading / have read* two novels so far this week.

5 They haven't *been writing / written* any other tests until now.

6 He *has been studying / has studied* in England and he's coming home next week.

7 I *have been making / have made* some coffee – does anybody want some?

8 Have you *sent / been sending* the parcel?

12 Choose the correct answer.

Eg *The garden and the house are completely white! It has .... all night!*
  a been snowed   **b** been snowing   **c** snowing

1 He .... finished his homework yet.
  a hasn't   **b** hasn't been   **c** has

2 We .... for the bus for half an hour and it still hasn't come!
  a have waited   **b** are waiting   **c** have been waiting

3 Sorry, but Mr Evans has just .... Can you phone again tomorrow?
  a left   **b** leaving   **c** been leaving

4 I .... seen Mary for weeks – do you think she is ill?
  a hasn't   **b** haven't   **c** have

5 Have you .... the news? They're having a baby!
  a been hearing   **b** heard   **c** hearing

6 They haven't been to the village .... a long time.
  a for   **b** since   **c** about

7 I've .... lunch so I'm not hungry, thank you.
  a had already   **b** already had   **c** already been having

8 Have you .... to Paris?
  a gone   **b** visited   **c** been

13 Complete the sentences in your own words.
Use the Present Perfect Simple or Continuous.

Eg   *I have been* ....*working hard all day*............ .

1   I haven't ....

2   Have you ....?

3   My mother has ....

4   Has she ....?

5   They haven't been ....

6   What have you ....?

Pairwork

Work with a partner. Take turns to ask and answer the following questions:

- Where have you been in your country?
- Where have you not been that you would like to go?
- Have you ever been abroad?
- Where did you go?

Writing

1   Write a short paragraph about the places you have been in your country and abroad. Write about the places you haven't been to.

2   Write a short paragraph about what you have been doing or what you have done today.

27

Past Perfect Simple

Affirmative

I/you had (I'd/you'd) stopped
he/she/it had (he'd/she'd/it'd) stopped
we/you/they had (we'd/you'd/they'd) stopped

Negative

I/you had not (hadn't) stopped
he/she/it had not (hadn't) stopped
we/you/they had not (hadn't) stopped

Question

Had I/you stopped?
Had he/she/it stopped?
Had we/you/they stopped?

Short answers

Yes, I/you had.   No, I/you hadn't.
Yes, he/she/it had.   No, he/she/it hadn't.
Yes, we/you/they had.   No, we/you/they hadn't.

The Past Perfect Simple is formed with the verb *had* + past participle of the main verb.

We use the Past Perfect Simple to talk about:

- an action that happened before another action in the past.
  Sam had studied hard for a month before he took his exams.
  Had Paula finished her homework before the film started?

- an action that happened before a specific time in the past.
  They had done the shopping before lunchtime.
  Linda had made the food for the party by four o'clock.

See the Irregular Verbs list on page 168.

Complete the sentences with the Past Perfect Simple.

Eg   I ....*had eaten*............ three biscuits before lunch. (eat)

1   They .... out very late the night before so they couldn't get up in the morning. (stay)

2   I .... at lots of pictures before I found one I really liked. (look)

3   .... before you fell asleep? (the film / finish)

4   The team were sad because they .... any other matches in the tournament. (not lose)

5   Dad .... his friends before he went out. (phone)

6   .... the restaurant when you got there? (they / already leave)

7   They .... their lunch by the time David came home from work. (have)

8   She .... all her jobs by nine o'clock so she left some for later. (not do)

Time Expressions with the Past Perfect Simple

after
already
as soon as
before
by (a time or date)
by the time
just ... when
never ... (before)
when

After we had been to the supermarket, we went home.
As soon as he had arrived at the airport, he checked in for his flight.
By the time Angela had woken up, it was lunchtime.
She had never seen a tiger before she went to Africa.

Notes
We use the word *by* to talk about an activity that had been completed before a specific time in the past.
He had eaten his lunch by two o'clock.

Past Perfect or Past Simple?

When we talk about two or more actions in the past, we use the Past Perfect Simple to emphasise that one action had finished before the other(s). For the other action(s), we use the Past Simple.
She had done all the ironing before she went out.
Before he went to school, he had taken the dog for a walk.

Write sentences using the words in brackets.

Eg   *The rain stopped. They went out for a walk (after)*
     After the rain had stopped, they went out for a walk.
     ....

1   The children finished their homework. It was nine o'clock. (by)
     ....

2   Nicola saved up her money. She went shopping. (before)
     ....

3   She finished talking on the phone. They had a meeting. (after)
     ....

4   The police got to the bank. The robbers had got away. (by the time)
     ....

5   She finished tidying the house. She invited her friends around. (as soon as)
     ....

6   They built their house in the village. They moved out of the city. (when)
     ....

7   We didn't go abroad. We went to Italy. (never ... before)
     ....

8   She turned the computer on. There was a power cut. (just ... when)
     ....

Past Perfect Continuous

Affirmative	Negative	Question
I had (I'd) been playing	I had not (hadn't) been playing	Had I been playing?
you had (you'd) been playing	you had not (hadn't) been playing	Had you been playing?
he had (he'd) been playing	he had not (hadn't) been playing	Had he been playing?
she had (she'd) been playing	she had not (hadn't) been playing	Had she been playing?
it had (it'd) been playing	it had not (hadn't) been playing	Had it been playing?
we had (we'd) been playing	we had not (hadn't) been playing	Had we been playing?
you had (you'd) been playing	you had not (hadn't) been playing	Had you been playing?
they had (they'd) been playing	they had not (hadn't) been playing	Had they been playing?

Short answers

Yes, I/you had.	No, I/you hadn't.
Yes, he/she/it had.	No, he/she/it hadn't.
Yes, you/we/they had.	No, you/we/they hadn't.

The Past Perfect Continuous is formed with *had + been +*
main verb + *-ing.*

We use the Past Perfect Continuous:

- to talk about an action that was in progress
  before another action in the past.
  *The garden looked beautiful because we had
  been working hard in it all weekend.*
  *Katie had been studying hard before her exams,
  so she did well.*

- to show that one action in the past lasted
  for a long time before another past action.
  *I had been looking for my watch for ages
  when Celia found it.*
  *She had been playing tennis for two hours so
  she had a shower.*

Complete the sentences with the Past Perfect Continuous.

Eg   They ....*had been driving*........ for two hours when the car broke down. *(drive)*

1   Mum .... the food in the oven when the guests arrived. (warm up)

2   Everyone .... such a nice time at the party it was a pity when it ended. (have)

3   I .... for two hours when I met a friend I hadn't seen for years. (shop)

4   We .... our compositions for very long when there was a loud crash. (not write)

5   She .... very well for weeks before she went into hospital. (not look)

6   The children .... happily when one of them started crying. (play)

7   He .... for the company for ten years before they made him manager. (work)

8   The tourists .... around Scotland by coach and were feeling exhausted. (travel)

9   Mike .... his homework properly so the teacher spoke to his parents. (not do)

10   I .... it for long when it stopped working! (not use)

Complete the questions with the Past Perfect Continuous.

Eg   ....*Had they been trying*........ to phone us all day? *(they / try)*

1   .... to the theatre when the accident happened? (she / drive)

2   What .... to do in the evening? (they / plan)

3   .... a lot of new clothes when I saw you? (you / buy)

4   .... a lot before the concert? She was very good. (she / practise)

5   .... in that house for a long time before the fire? (you / live)

6   .... for three days? There was so much food! (they / cook)

7   Who .... their products to? (they / sell)

8   Where .... him? (you / look for)

9   .... after lunch? (he / swim)

10   .... all night in the mountains? (it / snow)

Past Perfect Simple or Past Perfect Continuous?

We use both the Past Perfect Simple and the Past Perfect Continuous to show that one action had finished before another in the past. The difference is that we use the Past Perfect Continuous to emphasise the length of time an action lasted for.

Complete the text with the Past Simple, Past Perfect Simple or Past Perfect Continuous.

Last night my friends, Judy and Paul, (Eg) ....*told*.................. (tell) me all about the holiday which they (1) .... (have) at a wildlife sanctuary in southern India two years ago. They (2) .... (want) to go there for many years but they (3) .... (never have) enough money before. They (4) .... (save) up for three years before they finally (5) .... (go) on the trip last year.

The holiday organisers (6) .... (explain) to them before they (7) .... (arrive) there that they would spend the night in a campsite in the middle of the jungle, but when Judy (8) .... (hear) that snakes might come as visitors during the night she was a bit worried! The organisers (9) .... (not give) them that information before they (10) .... (book) the holiday!

In the end they (11) .... (have) a fantastic time though. When they (12) .... (come) back home, they (13) .... (tell) us how they (14) .... (see) elephants swimming, leopards hunting and lions sleeping in the hot sun. Obviously it (15) .... (be) the holiday of a lifetime!

6

Circle the correct answer.

Eg   *She* had been having / (had) *a nightmare last night because she had been watching a horror film on TV.*

1   He *had arrived / had been arriving* at the party a long time before anyone else came.
2   They had finished their lunch by the time Mum *had come / came* home.
3   When they got home from their holidays, they found that someone *broke / had broken* into their flat.
4   She *had been talking / had talked* on the phone for ages when the line went dead.
5   She was unhappy because she *had been losing / had lost* her gold chain.
6   They *waited / had been waiting* for a taxi for ages before they finally found one.
7   After the children *had been tidying / had tidied* their room, Mum came to have a look at it.
8   The fishermen *had caught / had been catching* a lot of fish and we bought some from the boat.

7

Complete the sentences with the words from the box.

| after   been   before   by   didn't   had (x2)   hadn't   soon |

Eg   *He hadn't ....been.......... listening to the teacher so he ....didn't.......... know what to do.*

1   They .... cooked the lunch by one o'clock.
2   We .... finished getting ready .... the time they came, so we missed the bus.
3   The boys .... been playing football all afternoon and they came home covered in mud.
4   As .... as the meeting had finished, everyone went home.
5   .... he had been swimming for an hour, he felt very tired.
6   Angela had put on her make-up .... she went out.

Last Saturday, I (Eg) ...._went_......... (go) with my friends to the fairground. By the evening, we (1) .... (be) on most of the rides and we (2) .... (spend) most of our money! My friends and I (3) .... (eat) hot dogs and ice creams all day and it (4) .... (be) nearly time to go home when we suddenly (5) .... (realise) that we (6) .... (not see) my dog, Rufus, for ages. He (7) .... (be) following us around all afternoon and evening, joining in the fun and he (8) .... (eat) some of our hot dogs! But now, he (9) .... (disappear)! Where (10) .... (he / go)?

We (11) .... (look) everywhere in the fairground but he (12) .... (not be) anywhere. I (13) .... (start) to feel a bit anxious because I (14) .... (love) Rufus and I certainly (15) .... (not want) to go home without him.

Just then, we (16) .... (hear) shouts coming from the Big Wheel. We all (17) .... (run) over there – and what (18) .... (we / see)? Rufus was sitting on one of the seats on the Big Wheel that (19) .... (be) up in the air and was now coming down again! Everyone was laughing and pointing at Rufus. I (20) .... (go) to get him off the wheel and we quickly (21) .... (disappear) into the crowd. When we (22) .... (get) home, nobody (23) .... (believe) me when I (24) .... (say) that Rufus (25) .... (be) on the Big Wheel all on his own!

Pairwork

Work with a partner. Take turns to ask and answer questions about what you had done before each of the times or days below. For example:

By eight o'clock this morning, Helen had eaten her breakfast.

- eight o'clock this morning
- ten o'clock last night
- two weeks ago
- last year
- last Saturday
- your last birthday

Writing

Write an entry in your diary for one day last week. Say what happened on that day, what had happened and what you had been doing before that day. Use the three tenses you have been practising in this unit.

33

Review 1 (Units 1–4)

1
Complete the sentences with the Present Simple.

Eg He ......*doesn't speak*...... Spanish. *(not speak)*.

1 .... from Spain? *(you / come)*
2 I .... in front of a computer every day. *(sit)*
3 They .... TV during the week. *(not watch)*
4 Snow .... when the sun shines. *(melt)*
5 .... jogging at the weekend? *(he / go)*
6 .... how much money they have got in the bank? *(they / know)*
7 They .... a lot of salad. *(not eat)*
8 .... cold in England in the winter? *(it / be)*

3
Complete the sentences with the verbs from the box. Use the Present Continuous.

| concentrate | eat | get | not live |
| make | plan | stay | wait | wash |

Eg My father ....*is eating*........ at the moment – can you ring back later?

1 Fortunately, my uncle .... better after his accident.
2 I .... Please don't interrupt me.
3 Dad .... the car at the moment.
4 He .... in England any more – he's gone to Italy.
5 .... you .... something special for his birthday?
6 I .... for you – are you ready?
7 .... he .... a model of a plane?
8 They .... with us for a few months.

2
Rewrite the sentences with the adverbs of frequency in the right place.

Eg *Does she phone her brother? (often)*
Does she often phone her brother?

1 Is she late for her appointments? *(always)*
....
....

2 He goes out for walks. *(rarely)*
....
....

3 I drive the car in the city. *(sometimes)*
....
....

4 Is it dangerous to go swimming straight after eating? *(always)*
....
....

5 He plays football in the summer. *(never)*
....
....

6 We see my cousins who live in Canada. *(rarely)*
....
....

7 Do you eat out in restaurants? *(often)*
....
....

8 She is ready to listen if you have a problem. *(usually)*
....
....

Circle the correct answer.

Eg   He (likes) / is liking *all sports, especially football.*

1   I *think* / *am thinking* that you're right.
2   She is a waitress. She *works* / *is working* very long hours.
3   That car *belongs* / *is belonging* to the manager.
4   We *stay* / *are staying* in a hotel until we can move into our new house.

5   I *am seeing* / *see* John tonight. We're going to the cinema.
6   I *can't hear* / *am not hearing* any noise at all.
7   It *is always raining* / *always rains* in the winter.
8   She *doesn't know* / *is not knowing* the answer.

Complete the sentences with the Past Simple.

Eg   I ...*didn't see*... him yesterday. *(not see)*

1   We .... any problems with the test. (not have)
2   She .... me a photo of their new house. (show)
3   Luckily, the baby .... all night long. (sleep)
4   .... on holiday in August? (you / go)
5   I .... my old teacher from primary school yesterday. (meet)
6   .... what they said last week? (they / mean)
7   It wasn't those boys who .... the window. (break)
8   .... those boots you saw in the sales? (you / buy)

Complete the sentences with the Past Continuous.

Eg   The students ...*were listening*... to the cassette this morning. *(listen)*

1   The shops .... very much last month but things are better now. (not sell)
2   The wind .... hard when they left the house. (blow)
3   I .... very fast but I soon got tired. (not run)
4   What .... at with your friend? (you / look)
5   We .... to London when we heard the news. (travel)
6   Who .... to on the phone? (you / talk)
7   They .... to phone us all day but we were out. (try)
8   She .... a very good time at the disco so she left early. (not have)

Complete the sentences with the verbs from the box. Use the correct form of **used to**.

chase	have	not know	like	play	practise	tell	travel	not walk

Eg   They ...*used to have*... two dogs but they don't have any pets now.

1   .... you .... abroad a lot?
2   He .... with toy soldiers when he was small.
3   We .... a lot but now we prefer it to driving or taking the bus.
4   He .... a lot of jokes but nobody laughed at them!
5   .... she .... playing with dolls?
6   Our dog .... cats but he's too old to do that now.
7   My mother .... anything about computers.
8   My sister .... the piano for three hours every day but she doesn't anymore.

Complete the sentences with the Present Perfect Simple.

Eg   He ...*hasn't written*... his composition yet. (not write)

1   They .... to buy him a present for his birthday! (forget)

2   There .... a lot of rain this month. (be)

3   .... all those books. (you / read)

4   We .... Jane recently? (not see)

5   She .... three coffees so far this morning. (have)

6   I .... here for ten years. (live)

7   They .... all the way from the train station and they're exhausted! (walk)

8   .... anything new recently? (you / buy)

Complete the sentences with the verbs from the box. Use the Present Perfect Continuous.

do	go	not live	look for	play
teach	think	try	work	

Eg   They .....*have been looking for*..... you all morning!

1   I .... to do this maths problem for an hour.

2   How long .... he .... in the garden?

3   They .... here very long.

4   She .... to the gym for three months now.

5   He .... at the village school since last year.

6   We .... about buying a new car.

7   I .... this job for ten months.

8   He .... football – that's why he's so muddy!

Choose the correct answer.

Eg   *I have .... for three hours and I still haven't finished.*
     a *worked*   **b** *been working*   **c** *working*

1   We .... all our jobs yet.
     a haven't   **b** haven't done   **c** have done

2   She .... for the competition for months.
     a has training   **b** is training   **c** has been training

3   No, Nick isn't here. He .... out to the shops.
     a has left   **b** has gone   **c** has been

4   Haven't you finished ....?
     a yet   **b** already   **c** just

5   She .... the bicycle. You can take it out for a ride if you want.
     a has been fixing   **b** already fixed   **c** has fixed

6   Have you .... tried water-skiing?
     a ever   **b** still   **c** before

7   I have lived in this house .... I was born.
     a always   **b** for   **c** since

8   Have you ever .... to Japan?
     a been   **b** visited   **c** gone

Complete the sentences with the Past Perfect Simple.

Eg I ....*had lost*.......... my glasses and I couldn't find them anywhere. *(lose)*

1 She .... her boyfriend before they went out. (phone)
2 .... the party when you got there? (they / leave)
3 We .... the children to school before it started to rain. (take)
4 .... their lunch before you got home? (they / have)
5 I still .... my work and it was midnight! (not finish)
6 He .... almost half of the cake by lunchtime! (eat)
7 .... the work by the time she arrived? (you / do)
8 I .... there before so I didn't know what to expect. (not go)

Complete the sentences with verbs from the box. Use the Past Perfect Continuous.

| eat | ice-skate | plan | play | rain | not study | win | walk | work |

Eg She ....*hadn't been studying*.......... very hard so I wasn't surprised when she failed her exams.

1 Where .... he ....? His clothes were very dirty.
2 .... you .... to change jobs?
3 It .... for three days before it finally stopped.
4 She .... sweets all morning – that's why she wasn't hungry.
5 They were wet because they .... in the rain.
6 The team .... the game until the other side scored.
7 I .... as a receptionist before I got the job as hotel manager.
8 He .... for the first time and his knees were covered in bruises!

Circle the correct answer.

Eg *He was happy because he* (had found) */ had been finding his watch.*

1 My friends *have been moving / moved* here last year.
2 They *looked / had been looking* for her all morning but they still hadn't found her by lunchtime.
3 When the children *had been studying / studied* for two hours, Mum said they could have a break.
4 Yesterday the postman *brought / had been bringing* a lot of letters for us!
5 I *had been cooking / had cooked* for the party for two days!
6 They *had started / had been starting* supper by the time Dad came home.
7 When they arrived at work on Monday morning, they found that someone *burgled / had burgled* the shop.
8 She *had been listening / had listened* to her new CD all evening before her mother told her to do her homework.

37

Future Tenses I

Present Continuous – Future Meaning

Affirmative

I am (I'm) travelling
you are (you're) travelling
he/she/it is (he's/she's/it's) travelling
we/you/they are (we're/you're/they're) travelling

Negative

I am (I'm not) travelling
you are not (aren't) travelling
he/she/it is not (isn't) travelling
we/you/they are not (aren't) travelling

Question

Am I travelling?
Are you travelling?
Is he/she/it travelling?
Are we/you/they travelling?

Short answers

Yes, I am.	No, I'm not.
Yes, you are.	No, you aren't.
Yes, he/she/it is.	No, he/she/it isn't.
Yes, we/you/they are.	No, we/you/they aren't.

We can use the Present Continuous to talk about plans and arrangements in the near future.
She's going away next week.
I'm playing tennis on Saturday.

1 Write sentences with the Present Continuous.

Eg   *I / cook / lunch / tomorrow*
.....*I am cooking lunch tomorrow.*............

1   I / meet / my new boss / on Monday
....
....

2   William / buy / a new car / at the weekend
....
....

3   She / stay / with her friends in England / next month
....
....

4   My brother / work / in the supermarket / on Saturday
....
....

5   He / leave / the USA / in the summer
....
....

6   We / fly / to Frankfurt / tomorrow
....
....

7   they / book / their summer holiday / tomorrow
....
....

8   They / have / a meeting / at three o'clock this afternoon
....
....

2 Write questions with the Present Continuous. Use the verbs in the box.

buy	decorate	do	go	have
help	make	repair	take	

Eg   ....*Is*.... he ....*decorating*.... his bedroom at the weekend?

1   .... Mum .... a special meal for your birthday tomorrow?

2   .... you .... a party on Friday?

3   .... she .... her friend with her on the trip?

4   .... they .... some new clothes next week?

5   .... Tonic .... Jim to clean the car later today?

6   .... he .... the shopping tomorrow?

7   .... we .... to the beach this afternoon?

8   .... you .... your bike at the weekend?

Present Simple – Future Meaning

Affirmative	**Negative**	**Question**
I/you travel	I/you do not (don't) travel	Do I/you travel?
he/she/it travels	he/she/it does not (doesn't) travel	Does he/she/it travel?
we/you/they travel	we/you/they do not (don't) travel	Do we/you/they travel?

Short answers

Yes, I/you do.	No, I/you don't.
Yes, he/she/it does.	No, he/she/it doesn't.
Yes, we/you/they do.	No, we/you/they don't.

We can use the Present Simple to talk about timetables and programmed events in the future.
The coach to Manchester leaves at eleven o'clock tomorrow morning.
The film doesn't begin until seven thirty tonight.

3 Complete the sentences with the Present Simple.

Eg   The bus from York ....*arrives*............ at five thirty this afternoon. (arrive)

1   The ship .... at seven o'clock tomorrow morning. (sail)
2   The train .... for another hour. (not leave)
3   The film .... at nine o'clock this evening. (start)
4   What time .... your plane ....? (take off)
5   My first helicopter lesson .... in half an hour! (begin)
6   The concert .... after midnight on Saturday, so we'll be home late. (finish)
7   The flight from America .... at eleven o'clock tonight. (land)
8   My friend's ferry .... at nine o'clock tomorrow morning. (arrive)

4 Make the sentences negative.

Eg   The theatre opens at six o'clock on Saturday.
      The theatre doesn't open at six o'clock on Saturday.
      ....

1   The Italian restaurant closes at midnight tonight.
      ....

2   Our English lesson starts at half past five tomorrow.
      ....

3   The plane to London takes off at nine o'clock this evening.
      ....

4   The train departs in half an hour.
      ....

5   The singers perform at eleven o'clock.
      ....

6   School starts at ten o'clock tomorrow morning.
      ....

Future Simple

Affirmative	Negative	Question
I/you will (I'll/you'll) travel	I/you will not (won't) travel	Will I/you travel?
he/she/it will (he'll/she'll/it'll) travel	he/she/it will not (won't) travel	Will he/she/it travel?
we/you/they will(we'll/you'll/they'll) travel	we/you/they will not (won't) travel	Will we/you/they travel?

Short answers

Yes, I/you will.	No, I/you won't.
Yes, he/she/it will.	No, he/she/it won't.
Yes, we/you/they will.	No, we/you/they won't.

We use the Future Simple for:

- predictions.
  I think she'll get that job she's applied for.

- decisions made at the time of speaking.
  That's the doorbell; I'll answer it.

- promises.
  I'll wash up every day for a month.
  Will you write to me every day?

- threats.
  Give me your money or I'll shoot!
  Be quiet or I'll call the police!

Notes
We only use *shall* with *I* and *we* in questions when we want to offer to do something or when we suggest something.
Shall I make supper tonight?
Shall we get a video for the evening?

---

5 Rewrite the sentences with **will** or **shall** in the correct place.

Eg *He be a great footballer by the time he's sixteen.*
He will be a great footballer by the time
he's sixteen.

1 I get you something to eat?
....
....

2 I think it be hot tomorrow.
....
....

3 Don't make a mess in your room or you not go out tonight!
....
....

4 I help you to peel the potatoes later, I promise.
....
....

THINK ABOUT IT!

*We can use **shall** instead of **will** for offers or suggestions with **I** and **we**.*

5 Look! It's snowing! I think I go for a walk.
....
....

6 You water my plants while I'm on holiday?
....

7 She not give the money back.
....
....

8 We play a different game now?
....
....

---

6 Choose the correct answer.

Eg *Don't worry, I won't / I'm not going to forget to post your letter.*

1 We *will go / are going* to the park to play football.
2 *Are you coming / Do you come* out with us on Saturday?
3 The show *will begin / begins* at eight o'clock.
4 'Does the train leave at seven?' 'Yes, it *does / is*.'
5 We *will have / are having* a meeting on Monday morning.
6 *Shall / Will* we go for a walk?
7 That exercise looks very difficult. I *will help / am helping* you with it.
8 We *are having / will have* a dinner party tomorrow night.

41

Be Going To

Affirmative

I am (I'm) going to travel
you are (you're) going to travel
he/she/it is (he's/she's/it's) going to travel
we/you/they are (we're/you're/they're) going to travel

Negative

I am not (I'm not) going to travel
you are not (aren't) going to travel
he/she/is not (isn't) going to travel
we/you/they are not (aren't) going to travel

Question

Am I going to travel?
Are you going to travel?
Is he/she/it going to travel?
Are we/you/they going to travel?

Short answers

Yes, I am.   No, I'm not.
Yes, you are.   No, you aren't.
Yes, he/she/it is.   No, he/she/it isn't.
Yes, we/you/they are.   No, we/you/they aren't.

We use *be going to* talk about:

■ plans and arrangements in the near future.
We are going to stay on a farm for our holiday this summer.

■ something we know is going to happen because we have evidence.
Be careful! That glass is going to fall.

Notes

We can use both *be going to* and the Present Continuous to talk about plans and arrangements.
I'm going to visit my friend tomorrow.
I'm visiting my friend tomorrow.

---

7 Complete the sentences with the correct form of **be going to** and a verb from the box.

build	buy	fail	have	live
snow	start	study	travel	

Eg   He ......*is going to buy*...... a new house
      next year.

1   They .... languages at
    university.

2   Dad .... going to the
    gym because he's overweight.

3   David and Jill .... their
    own house when they save up enough money.

4   I .... a shower
    and go to bed.

5   Where ....you .... after
    you're married?

6   You .... all your exams
    if you don't study harder.

7   We .... round Australia
    for twelve months when we finish university.

8   Look at the sky! It ....
    ....!

8 Write questions and answers using the verbs in brackets.

Eg *you / sell / your house / next week (decorate)*
....
Are you going to sell your house next week?
....
No, I'm going to decorate it.

1 they / buy / the birthday cake / later today (make)
....
....
....

2 she / learn / Italian / next year (teach)
....
....
....

3 we / earn / some money / in the summer (spend)
....
....
....

4 the doctor / examine / the patient / this evening (visit)
....
....
....

5 you / read / the e-mail / today (send)
....
....
....

6 he / drive / around Europe / next summer (sail)
....
....
....

7 I / buy / the presents / for my birthday (receive)
....
....
....

8 Peter / wash / the walls (paint)
....
....
....

9 Complete the sentences with the correct form of **be going to** or the Future Simple.

Eg I ....*am going to make*.... (make) a coffee. ....*Shall I make*.... (make) one for you?

1 Brian .... Art at college. Do you think he .... a famous artist one day? (study, be)

2 I .... to town this afternoon. I promise I .... you something nice back! (go, bring)

3 It .... a lovely day – .... you .... me wash the car later? (be, help)

4 David .... the drinks now. I .... a glass of wine, please. (order, have)

5 '................................ you .... to the barbecue at the weekend?'
   'I don't know. I .... on Friday night.' (come, decide)

6 'Charlie is eating too much chocolate. He .... very sick in a minute!'
   'Then I .... him a drink of water.' (feel, bring)

7 'We're late. We .... the bus!'
   'Never mind. We .... a taxi.' (miss, take)

8 '................................ you .... me tonight?'
   'No, I .... visit my cousins.' (phone, visit)

10 Choose the correct answer.

Eg   *The flight to Rio de Janiero* .... *in two hours.*
    a *leaving*   **b** *leaves*   **c** *will be leave*

1   What .... at the weekend?
    a you do   **b** are you doing   **c** will you do

2   I don't think this party .... much fun.
    a will be   **b** is being   **c** is going to

3   .... buy a new pair of jeans today?
    a Are you   **b** Will you be   **c** Are you going to

4   He .... to the doctor this evening about his health problems.
    a is going to   **b** is going   **c** will go

5   The baseball instructor .... explain the rules of the game before you start playing.
    a is   **b** will   **c** does

6   Mum .... the children to the Science Museum next Saturday.
    a is taking   **b** will to take   **c** takes

7   That bag looks heavy. .... I carry it for you?
    a Do   **b** Shall   **c** Am

8   She looks very pale. I think she .... faint.
    a will   **b** shall   **c** is going to

11 Complete the dialogue with one word in each gap.

Joe: What (Eg) ....*are*....... you doing at the weekend, Kate?

Kate: Nothing much. What about you?

Joe: I'm (1) .... to go to the Robbie Williams concert. My brother bought me two tickets for my birthday.

Kate: Lucky you! I'm sure you (2) .... both enjoy the concert a lot.

Joe: Yes, I think it (3) .... be a brilliant concert. But my brother (4) .... not coming with me.

Kate: Why not?

Joe: He's (5) .... out with his girlfriend tomorrow.

Kate: So, you're (6) .... to go on your own?

Joe: No, I (7) .... taking a friend.

Kate: That (8) .... be nice. Who (9) .... you giving the ticket to?

Joe: You! (10) .... you come to the concert with me?

Kate: Me? Yes, I'd love to come! What time (11) .... the concert start?

Joe: It (12) .... at nine o'clock so I (13) .... pick you up at half past eight.

Kate: Fantastic! I (14) .... see you tomorrow!

12 Find the mistakes and write the sentences correctly.

Eg   *My flight to Sydney taking off at nine this evening.*
      My flight to Sydney takes off at nine this evening.

1   Are you go anywhere nice tonight?

   ....

2   I'm thirsty. I think I'm going to have some water.

   ....

3   Shall you help me carry the shopping, please?

   ....

4   I'm sure you won't to fail your exams.

   ....

5   Which planets are astronauts going exploring in the next century?

   ....

6   'Are you going swimming on Saturday?' 'No, I won't.'

   ....

Pairwork

Work with a partner. Take turns to ask each other questions about the future.
For example:

- What will your town or city be like in the year 2200?
- What do you think is going to happen to our planet in two hundred years?
- What are your friends and family doing tomorrow?

Writing

Write a magazine article about what you think life will be like on Earth in the year
2200. Use your answers from Pairwork above to help you.

The future

   ....
   ....
   ....
   ....
   ....
   ....
   ....
   ....
   ....
   ....

Future Tenses II

What will you be doing while I'm at work today, Tonic. Will you be busy?

Yes, I'll be very busy. I'll be cleaning the house, I'll be doing the ironing and I'll be making your supper!

Future Continuous

Affirmative	Negative	Question
I will (I'll) be working	I will not (won't) be working	Will I be working?
you will (you'll) be working	you will not (won't) be working	Will you be working?
he will (he'll) be working	he will not (won't) be working	Will he be working?
she will (she'll) be working	she will not (won't) be working	Will she be working?
it will (it'll) be working	it will not (won't) be working	Will it be working?
we will (we'll) be working	we will not (won't) be working	Will we be working?
you will (you'll) be working	you will not (won't) be working	Will you be working?
they will (they'll) be working	they will not (won't) be working	Will they be working?

Short answers

Yes, I/you will.	No, I/you won't.
Yes, he/she/it will.	No, he/she/it won't.
Yes, we/you/they will.	No, we/you/they won't.

We use the Future Continuous to talk about something that will be in progress at a specific time in the future.
This time next week, we will be sailing to France.
Will they be dancing at ten o'clock on Saturday night?

1 Complete the sentences with the Future Continuous.

Eg   Tomorrow morning I ....will be taking....... an English exam. (take)

1   This time next week they .... to New Zealand. (travel)

2   At four o'clock this afternoon she .... to the radio. (listen)

3   Tomorrow afternoon you .... pizza at my house! (eat)

4   Next Monday morning he .... to Thailand. (fly)

5   I .... in a bank from next week. (work)

6   In two hours we .... the Ricky Martin concert. (watch)

7   He .... basketball all Saturday afternoon. (play)

8   I .... on the beach next week. (lie)

2 Make the sentences negative.

Eg   They will be doing their homework this evening.
   They won't be doing their homework this evening.
   ....

1   You will be writing that composition all afternoon.
   ....

2   Tonic will be working hard while Jim is at work.
   ....

3   I'll be waiting outside the cinema at two o'clock.
   ....

4   We'll be taking our driving test on Saturday.
   ....

5   Tourists will be sunbathing on the moon next year.
   ....

6   People will be living on other planets in ten years' time.
   ....

3 Write questions.

Eg   you / work / in an office / next year / ?
   Will you be working in an office next year?
   ....

1   they / sleep / at midnight / ?
   ....

2   he / paint / the house / all day / ?
   ....

3   you / write / e-mails / for three hours / ?
   ....

4   you / think / about me / when you're on holiday / ?
   ....

5   Mum / make / dinner / when / we get home / ?
   ....

6   the children / ride / their bikes / this afternoon / ?
   ....

4 Write questions and answers using the verbs in brackets.

Eg *they / dance / at the party (sing)*
    Will they be dancing at the party?
    No, they won't. They'll be singing at the party.

1   you / read / for the next hour (write)

    ....

    ....

2   he / repair / the car / all afternoon (clean)

    ....

    ....

3   we / sail / to France / this time tomorrow (fly)

    ....

    ....

4   the teacher / give out / the tests / this afternoon (mark)

    ....

    ....

5   she / dig / the garden / at seven o'clock / this evening (water)

    ....

    ....

6   the students / relax / all day (study)

    ....

    ....

7   you / walk / to work / tomorrow (drive)

    ....

    ....

8   he / have / a party / on Saturday (go to)

    ....

    ....

5 Complete the sentences with the Future Continuous. Use the verbs from the box.

| lie | not buy | not drive | not go | not have | not sing | study | wear | work |

Eg *It's raining. We* .... *won't be having* .... *a picnic this afternoon.*

1   She has a sore throat. She .... in the concert tomorrow night.

2   He's lost his wallet. He .... any new CDs this weekend.

3   Dad's very busy. He .... until nine o'clock this evening.

4   I've got an exam tomorrow. I .... all night!

5   I'll meet you at the airport. I .... a red jacket so you will easily recognise me.

6   There's no snow in Austria, so we .... on a skiing holiday this month.

7   His car has broken down. He .... to work this week.

8   Today is the last day of school. This time tomorrow I .... in bed!

6 Write sentences.

Anne's diary - tomorrow

9 am	make breakfast
11 am	clean my room
1 pm	write e-mails
2 pm	eat lunch
4 pm	dye my hair
5 pm	cut the grass
7 pm	watch TV
9 pm	cook supper
11 pm	have a shower

Eg *At 9 am tomorrow Anne will be making breakfast.*

1 ....

2 ....

3 ....

4 ....

5 ....

6 ....

7 ....

8 ....

Future Simple or Future Continuous?

We use the Future Simple to talk about something (a prediction, an offer, a sudden decision, a promise) that will happen and be completed in the future.
I think you'll live to a very old age.
I'll help you with those boxes.

We use the Future Continuous to talk about something that will be in progress at a specific time in the future.
This time tomorrow, we'll be writing our maths test.
What will you be doing at eight o'clock tonight?

7 Complete the sentences with the Future Simple or the Future Continuous.

Eg I'm sure it ....*will be*............ sunny tomorrow. (be)

1 On Monday evening she .... in the concert. (play)

2 I know they .... their beds before they go out. (not make)

3 .... you .... the washing up for me? (finish)

4 Don't phone me at eleven o'clock. I .... a meeting. (have)

5 I don't feel well. I think I .... down for half an hour. (lie)

6 What .... you .... on Saturday night? (do)

7 .... you always .... my friend? (be)

8 How many people .... on Earth in 2500? (live)

9 By this time next week they .... on the beach. (relax)

10 If he's lucky he .... his driving test. (pass)

THINK ABOUT IT!

Will the action be in progress in the future? Use the Future Continuous.

49

8 Complete the sentences with the words from the box.

| be | compete | competing | take | taking | watch | watching | will | won't |

Eg ....Will........................ you help me with my homework later on?

1 They'll .... having breakfast at eight o'clock tomorrow morning.

2 I'm quite sure it .... rain tomorrow, so let's arrange to go to the beach.

3 Everybody will be .... the football match on Saturday.

4 Where will the Olympics .... place in 2008?

5 Which teams will be .... in the final competition?

6 At nine o'clock tomorrow I'll be .... my English exam.

7 He'll .... in the Olympics when he's older.

8 You go and play tennis and I'll .... you.

9 Choose the correct answer.

Eg *Will the youth orchestra .... at the summer concert?*
   a *perform*   **(b)** *be performing*   **c** *will perform*

1 Do you think people .... electric cars in the future?
   a will driving   **b** to drive   **c** will drive

2 On Saturday evening we will .... to America.
   a fly   **b** be flying   **c** flying

3 The weatherman says that it .... foggy this evening.
   a will   **b** will being   **c** will be

4 What do you think you .... at five o'clock tomorrow afternoon?
   a do   **b** will be doing   **c** will do

5 I promise I .... home before you go to bed.
   a will be being   **b** will be   **c** be

6 .... always love me?
   a Will   **b** Will you   **c** You will

7 That looks difficult! .... you?
   a Shall I help   **b** Shall I be helping   **c** Shall help

8 .... next week she will be climbing Mount Everest.
   a This time   **b** Soon   **c** At

10 Complete the text with the words from the box.

| be | by | cook | staying | studying | this | will (x2) | won't |

On Saturday my parents are going on holiday to France – (Eg) ....by........................ this time next week they will be (1) .... in an expensive hotel and they will (2) .... learning to speak French. I (3) .... be with them because I'll be (4) .... hard for my exams. My grandmother (5) .... be staying with me. She will (6) .... all the meals and clean the house while my parents are away.

(7) .... time next year I will be one year older and it (8) .... be my last year. No more school! No more exams! Lucky me!

11 Find the mistakes and write the sentences correctly.

Eg *What will you doing ten years from now?*
    What will you be doing ten years from now?
    ....

1   Will you be helping me to do the ironing, please?
    ....

2   What time will you be being home this evening?
    ....

3   At nine o'clock this evening will you work?
    ....

4   I'm very hungry. I think I'll be having a sandwich.
    ....

5   Do you think it will rain when we get up in the morning?
    ....

6   How often you visit your parents after you're married?
    ....

7   Will you to be working on Easter Monday?
    ....

8   I'll be doing that for you!
    ....

Pairwork

Work with a partner. Take turns to ask and answer questions about the future. Think about:

- what you will be doing this time next year.
- where you will be at Christmas and at Easter next year.
- what you will be doing at seven o'clock on Saturday night.
- what you think the weather will be like next week.

Writing

Write a short paragraph about what you think your life will be like ten years from now. Use the Future Continuous. Think about:

- which city you will be living in
- what kind of house you will be living in
- what you will be studying
- what your family and friends will be doing

In the year ...., ten years from now, I will be ....

....

....

....

....

....

....

....

Countable and Uncountable Nouns

Countable Nouns

Most nouns are countable and have a singular and plural form.

table	→	tables
lady	→	ladies
toy	→	toys
dress	→	dresses
knife	→	knives
person	→	people

We don't use *a* or *an* before a plural noun. We can use the word *some* in an affirmative sentence and the word *any* in a question or a negative sentence.

I've got a cake. → We've got some cakes.
Has he got any brothers? → No, he hasn't got any brothers.

Notes

When we offer or ask for something, we use the word *some*, not *any*.
Would you like some grapes?
Can I have some biscuits, please?

Uncountable Nouns

There are other nouns which are uncountable. They do not have a plural form.

fruit	homework	information
salt	money	knowledge
cheese	music	news
water	weather	progress
milk	equipment	time
food	furniture	rubbish
chocolate	luggage	traffic

All uncountable nouns are followed by a singular verb.
This music is lovely.

We don't use *a* or *an* with uncountable nouns. We can use the word *some* in affirmative sentences and the word *any* in questions and negative sentences.
I would like some wine with my food, please.
Have you got any money with you? No, I haven't got any money.

When we offer or ask for something, we use the word *some*, not *any*.
Would you like some more coffee?
Could I have some milk, please?

We can 'count' uncountable nouns by using phrases of quantity.

bread	*a loaf of bread*	*three loaves of bread*
coffee	*a cup of coffee*	*three cups of coffee*
cola	*a can of cola*	*three cans of cola*
jam	*a jar of jam*	*three jars of jam*
milk	*a carton of milk*	*three cartons of milk*
rice	*a bowl of rice*	*three bowls of rice*
soup	*a tin of soup*	*three tins of soup*
sugar	*a bag of sugar*	*three bags of sugar*
tea	*a packet of tea*	*three packets of tea*
water	*a glass of water*	*three glasses of water*
wine	*a bottle of wine*	*three bottles of wine*

1 Complete the sentences with **some** or **any**.

Eg   *Have you bought .... fruit for the picnic?*

1   I saw .... money on the table – is it yours?
2   Are there .... biscuits in the cupboard?
3   Would you like .... wine with your meal?
4   Can you give me .... information about trains to Inverness, please?
5   Is there .... rubbish to go in the bin?

6   We haven't had .... news about grandma from the hospital today.
7   Do you want .... food or just a cup of tea?
8   Are there .... bottles of water in the fridge?
9   There isn't .... furniture in Sue's new flat.
10   I saw .... interesting news on the television.

2 Tick (✓) the correct sentence.

Eg   *There isn't some good music on the radio at the moment.* __
     There isn't any good music on the radio at the moment. ✓

1   He made good progresses at school this year. __
    He made good progress at school this year. __

2   There isn't any traffic on the motorway. __
    There isn't some traffic on the motorway. __

3   Do you want any ketchup on your sandwich? __
    Do you want some ketchup on your sandwich? __

4   Have you got any wine? __
    Have you got some wine? __

5   There is some chocolate in the fridge. __
    There are some chocolate in the fridge. __

6   He's got some luggage for his journey. __
    He's got any luggage for his journey. __

7   Would you like some fruit after the meal? __
    Would you like some fruits after the meal? __

8   Please buy two breads from the baker's. __
    Please buy two loaves of bread from the baker's. __

53

Quantifiers - A Little / A Few / A Lot Of

We use *a little* with uncountable nouns to say that a small amount of something exists.
There's only a little wine left in my glass.

We use *a few* with plural countable nouns to say that a small number of something exists.
We can use of with a few.
There are a few people waiting for the train.
A few of my friends will be coming to the party.

We use *a lot of* with uncountable and plural countable nouns. We usually use it in affirmative sentences.
She's got a lot of luggage to carry.
There are a lot of interesting books in the library.

3 Choose the correct answer.

Eg *I haven't got* .... *homework this evening.*
    a little   **b** a lot of   **c** a few

1   There were .... good reports on the news this evening.
    a a little   **b** any   **c** a few

2   There might be .... rain later on today.
    a a few   **b** a lot   **c** a little

3   He'll need .... luck if he's going to pass his English exam!
    a a lot of   **b** a few   **c** little

4   Will you put .... salt in the soup?
    a a few   **b** some   **c** little

5   We need .... packets of coffee.
    a three   **b** a little   **c** any

6   Were there .... people at the concert?
    a a lot of   **b** little   **c** a few

7   We still have .... time left.
    a a little   **b** a lot   **c** a few

8   Get .... cans of coke while you're at the shop.
    a a little   **b** some of   **c** a few

Much / Many & Not Enough

We use *much* with uncountable nouns in negative sentences and questions.
I haven't got much information about computers.
Is there much money in your bank account?

We use *many* with plural countable nouns. We usually use it in negative sentences and questions.
There aren't many biscuits left.
Were there many people on the train this morning?

We use *too much* with uncountable nouns and *too many* with plural countable nouns to talk about a quantity that is more than we need or want.
There's too much rubbish on the streets.
There are too many people who throw rubbish in the streets.

We use *not enough* with both uncountable nouns and plural countable nouns to talk about a quantity that is less than we need or want.
There isn't enough money in my bank account to pay for this holiday.
There aren't enough places for us to go in this town.

Complete the sentences with **much**, **many** or **not enough**.

Eg   How ....*much*............ luggage are you taking on holiday with you?

1   How .... bags can we take on the plane?
2   There are .... chairs for everyone to sit on.
3   She hasn't got .... clothes.
4   I can't pay for your drink because I haven't got .... money.
5   He's got too .... homework to do tonight.
6   There are too .... rules in English grammar!
7   There is .... time to finish the work.
8   He hasn't made .... progress at college this term.
9   You paid too .... money for those trainers.
10   Is there .... rubbish outside?

THINK ABOUT IT!

*We use **much** with Uncountable Nouns and **many** with Countable Nouns. We use **not enough** with both!*

Both / Either / Neither / All / None

We use *both, either* and *neither* to talk about two people or things.

Both means *one and the other.*
Both of them go to that school.
He likes both rock and reggae music.

Either means *one or the other.*
I don't think either of the children go to that school.
I listen to either rock or reggae music.

Neither means *not one and not the other.*
Neither of the boys goes to that school.
His sister enjoys neither rock nor reggae music.

We use *all* and *none* to talk about more than two people or things. *All* means *every one of them. None* means *not even one of them.*
All the students in my class passed their final exam.
None of my friends play chess.

Choose the correct answer.

Eg   We visited *both* / neither *Italy and Spain when we toured Europe last summer.*

1   You can have *neither / either* the spaghetti bolognese or the pizza.
2   *All / Either* of the people I met in France last year have sent me e-mails.
3   I'm not sure who broke the window. It was *either / both* Paul or John.
4   Plant *all / none* the flowers in the garden – they'll look nice.
5   *None / Either* of the people in my family can speak Italian.
6   My friend and I are *either / neither* going to the USA or to Asia next summer.
7   *Neither / All* of my parents wants to live anywhere except England.
8   *None / Neither* of the football fans were happy with the result.
9   They are *neither / all* going to help with the gardening.
10   Stop talking, *none / all* of you!

Complete the sentences with the words from the box.

| a few | a lot of | both | either | enough |
| many | much | neither | none |

Eg There are only .... a few .... apples and oranges left in the bowl.

1 There isn't .... wine for us all to have a glass.

2 I can offer you .... cake or ice cream for dessert.

3 We had .... fun on the beach yesterday.

4 I think I put too .... salt in the soup.

5 My mum and dad are .... good skiers.

6 .... of the people in my English class have ever been to London.

7 I don't think there are .... people in Spain who can speak Japanese.

8 .... I nor my brother understands German.

Articles

The Indefinite Article – a / an

We use the indefinite article with:

- singular countable nouns that we talk about for the first time.
  I can see a red Ferrari.

- nouns that talk about someone's job, nationality, religion or political beliefs.
  He's a computer programmer.
  Is she an American?
  I am a Conservative.

- certain numbers instead of *one* and in some quantifying phrases.
  a hundred
  a million
  once a week
  fifty kilometres an hour

We do not use the indefinite article with:

- plural countable nouns.
  Ferraris are great cars.

- uncountable nouns.
  There is cheese in the fridge.

- adjectives that are not followed by a noun.
  He's nasty. (He's a nasty man.)

- names of meals (except when there is an adjective before them).
  When do you want breakfast?
  Let's have a cooked breakfast.

Complete the sentences with **a**, **an** or **–**.

Eg I'm sure that man is .... a .... doctor.

1 .... children don't like being told what to do.

2 I've saved .... hundred Euros this month.

3 You mustn't drive faster than eighty kilometres .... hour on this road.

4 That was .... lovely lunch, thank you.

5 What .... nice hair you've got!

6 What are we having for .... dinner tonight?

7 Is Bill Clinton .... Democrat?

8 It's good for you to eat .... apple every day.

Articles

The Definite Article – *the*

We use the definite article:

■ with singular and plural countable nouns and with uncountable nouns.
The cake is finished.
The cakes are finished.
The coffee is delicious.

■ when we talk about someone or something that has already been mentioned in a previous sentence.
I met a man and a woman at the party. The man was friendly, but the woman wasn't.

■ when we talk about someone or something specific.
The girl with the red dress is my best friend.

■ with nouns which are thought of as being unique.
The Earth goes round the sun.

■ with names of seas *(the Red Sea)*, rivers *(the Amazon)*, mountain ranges *(the Himalayas)*, oceans *(the Pacific Ocean)* and deserts *(the Sahara)*.

■ with names of hotels *(the Holiday Inn)*, theatres *(the Globe Theatre)*, cinemas *(the Odeon Cinema)*, ships *(the Titanic)*, newspapers *(the Express)* and organisations *(the World Wildlife Fund)*.

■ with groups of islands and countries in the plural.
We had a wonderful time in the Canary Islands last summer.
I studied in the United States of America.

■ with nationalities, musical instruments and family names.
The Chinese eat with chopsticks.
I'm learning to play the guitar.
Do you know the Browns?

■ with titles of people (without names).
Who is the chairman of this committee?

■ with the superlative form of adjectives.
She's the prettiest girl in the class.

■ with numbers showing frequency and the words *last* and *only*.
That's the third time he's been late for work this week.
This is the last thing to go in the suitcase.
He's the only man I could love.

■ with dates and the words *morning*, *afternoon* and *evening*.
I'm getting married on 5th September.
(We say the fifth of September.)
I'll go to the supermarket in the afternoon.

We do not use the definite article with:

■ plural countable nouns when we talk in general.
Lions are hunters.

■ names of people, roads, cities, islands, countries or continents.
His name is George.
I live in Prince's Street.
Mark is in Rome this week.
Have you ever been to Barbados?
I've never been to India.
Europe is a big continent.

■ abstract nouns.
Love is a wonderful thing.

■ the words *hospital, church, bed, home, prison, work* and *school*.
What time will you be home tonight?

■ names of meals.
What shall we have for supper?

■ names of languages when we don't say the word *language*.
Japanese is very difficult.
The Japanese language is very difficult.

■ titles of people when we say their name.
Prince Charles is the father of Prince William.

8 Complete the sentences with **the** or **–**.

Eg *Have you read a lot about ....the.... ancient Greeks?*

1 How many of .... Balearic Islands have you been to?
2 .... beauty is not as important as .... honesty.
3 My father plays .... guitar.
4 They went to .... Grand Canyon when they visited .... America.
5 .... Sheraton Hotel is in .... Regent Street.
6 We're inviting .... Greens and .... John and Freda Williams to the party.
7 Why has he been sent to .... prison?
8 Where are we going after .... lunch?
9 Do you speak .... French?
10 Do you know who .... Queen of England is?

10 Find the mistakes and write the sentences correctly.

Eg *He is a most patient man I know.*
   He is the most patient man I know.
   ....

1 Do you know where a Queen's Hotel is?
   ....
   ....
2 Dad is still in the bed.
   ....
   ....
3 Are you enjoying studying the English?
   ....
   ....
4 They first met on holiday in Canary Islands.
   ....
   ....
5 Was your grandfather the doctor?
   ....
   ....
6 Policeman is searching for clues.
   ....
   ....
7 The Prime Minister Blair made a speech.
   ....
   ....
8 The giraffes have very long necks.
   ....
   ....

9 Complete the sentences with **a**, **an** or **the**.

Eg *How long has he lived in ....the.... United States of America?*

1 Have you seen .... man who owns that motorbike?
2 I think I want .... sandwich and .... drink now.
3 Where is .... restaurant you went to last Saturday?
4 Did you know astronauts are hoping to land on .... planet Mars before long?
5 He rowed all the way across .... English Channel on his own.
6 Have you got .... pen I could borrow, please?
7 I'd hate to be stuck in .... Arizona Desert without any water!
8 I'll have .... orange instead of cake for my dessert.

11 Find the extra word and write it in the space.

Eg *My father reads and The Observer every day. ..and..*

1 You've got the beautiful eyes! ....
2 Be quiet. I've got a work to do. ....
3 The criminal will stay in the prison for a very long time. ....
4 He's the only a man I know who can play the violin. ....
5 We have to go to a school every day during term time. ....
6 Do you like the cats as pets? ....
7 I spent my holidays in the France. ....
8 Do you want a milk in your coffee? ....

Complete the text with **a, an, the** or **–**.

On Monday we had (Eg) ..*an*.. English lesson with (1) .... Mrs Green. (2) .... lesson is usually on (3) .... Friday but she was ill last week. She told us all about (4) .... London and (5) .... England, where she went last year for her summer holidays. She speaks very good (6) .... English so she had no trouble talking to people and getting around. It was (7) .... second time she had been there and she said that it was (8) .... best holiday she had ever had.

She stayed at (9) .... Kensington Hotel, she went to (10) .... Royal Palace Theatre and she took (11) .... boat trip on (12) .... River Thames. (13) .... most interesting thing about her trip was the day she visited (14) .... Buckingam Palace. She didn't see (15) .... Queen though!

During the second week of her holiday, she went on a day trip to (16) .... France. She was scared of going through the Channel Tunnel so she took (17) .... ferry across (18) .... English Channel instead.

This year she isn't going to England. She's going to (19) .... Greece and she's going to visit some of (20) .... Ionian Islands.

Pairwork

Look inside your bag and talk to your partner about what is inside it.
For example:

There is a pen and some pencils.
The pen is blue and the pencils are black.
There are some books.

Writing

Write a short paragraph describing your bedroom. Try to use as many of the words in the box as possible. For example:

In my bedroom there is a bed and a desk. Both of them are made of wood. There are some bookshelves near the bed.

a	a few	a little	all	a lot of	an	any	both	either
many	much	neither	none	not enough	some	the		

....
....
....
....
....
....
....
....
....
....

59

Future Perfect Simple

Future Perfect Simple

Affirmative	Negative	Question
I will (I'll) have eaten	I will not (won't) have eaten	Will I have eaten?
you will (you'll) have eaten	you will not (won't) have eaten	Will you have eaten?
he will (he'll) have eaten	he will not (won't) have eaten	Will he have eaten?
she will (she'll) have eaten	she will not (won't) have eaten	Will she have eaten?
it will (it'll) have eaten	it will not (won't) have eaten	Will it have eaten?
we will (we'll) have eaten	we will not (won't) have eaten	Will we have eaten?
you will (you'll) have eaten	you will not (won't) have eaten	Will you have eaten?
they will (they'll) have eaten	they will not (won't) have eaten	Will they have eaten?

Short answers

Yes, I/you will.	No, I/you won't.
Yes, he/she/it will.	No, he/she/it won't.
Yes, we/you/they will.	No, we/you/they won't.

We use the Future Perfect Simple to talk about something that will be complete before something else happens or before a specific time in the future.

(It's five o'clock and I'm doing my homework. I will be doing my homework for another hour and a half.)
By seven o'clock I will have finished my homework.

(It's already 9 pm. David still has a lot of work to do.)
David won't have finished his work before he goes to bed.

1 Complete the sentences with the Future Perfect Simple.

Like other future tenses, the form
of the Future Perfect Simple is the
same for every person:
will + have + past participle.

Eg   Dad ....*will have dug*.......... the garden before Mum arrives home. (dig)

1   They .... their beds before they have breakfast. (make)
2   She .... a shower before she goes to work. (have)
3   I .... this book before I go to bed tonight. (finish)
4   It .... at least once before next summer. (snow)
5   You .... more than fifty compositions before you leave school. (write)
6   We .... forty kilometres before it gets dark. (ride)
7   He .... all his friends e-mails before tomorrow morning. (send)
8   Mum .... to work before I get up tomorrow. (go)

2 Write questions.

Eg   He will have lost his new mobile phone before the
     weekend.
     Will he have lost his new mobile phone
     before the weekend?

1   Doctors will have found a cure for cancer before
    the 22nd century.
    ....
    ....

2   Astronauts will have walked on Mars before the
    end of this century.
    ....
    ....

3   Dogs will have learnt how to use computers
    before the year 2010.
    ....
    ....

4   He will have travelled to India before he goes to
    university.
    ....
    ....

5   Firemen will have put out the forest fire before it
    gets dark tonight.
    ....
    ....

3 Make negative sentences.

Eg   he / earn / enough money / for a new car /
     before he's twenty
     He won't have earned enough money for a
     new car before he's twenty.

1   they / buy / a house / before they're married
    ....
    ....

2   her baby / learn / how to talk / before it's three
    months old
    ....
    ....

3   she / make / the dinner / before four o'clock
    ....
    ....

4   we / see / news / before we go out
    ....
    ....

5   you / drink / all that milk / before you go to bed
    ....
    ....

6   he / take / his university exams / before he's
    fourteen
    ....
    ....

Time Expressions with the Future Perfect

before ...	by Wednesday
by five o'clock	by the weekend
by next week	in a year's time
by now	in ten minutes
by the time ...	soon

Complete the sentences with **by** or **in**.

Eg   *He will have lived here for ten years ......by..... next summer.*

1   I will have left school .... two years.
2   .... this evening she will have learnt all her English grammar.
3   They will have finished their dinner .... half an hour.
4   The doctor will have examined twenty patients .... the time she leaves work.
5   Will you have bought your own house .... two year's time?
6   I think I will have passed all my exams .... next summer.
7   She won't have got married .... six months.
8   Will he have cleaned the car .... the weekend?

5   Complete the sentences with the Future Perfect. Use the verbs in the box.

discover   do   find   finish   have   host   learn   think   win

Eg   *By eight o'clock this evening I ....will have done........ all the ironing.*

1   He .... a new job by next month.
2   .... you .... how to drive by next summer?
3   Scientists .... new ways of making energy by the year 2500.
4   The chef .... of lots more unusual recipes by this time next year.
5   Colin Jackson .... more medals by the year 2005.
6   Greece .... the Olympic Games by 2005.
7   His computer course .... by the end of August.
8   I .... another birthday by this time next year.

THINK
ABOUT IT!

In order to be good at the Future Perfect Simple you have to know the past participles of irregular verbs very well. Use the table on page 168 to learn them.

6   Write the words in the correct order.

Eg   *married / we / been / by September / will / for ten years / have*
We will have been married for ten years by September.

1   have / you / your house / will / by Christmas / built / ?
....

2   had / go out / I / before / will / a bath / I / have
....

3   have / won't / he / before / read / to work / goes / the newspaper / he
....

4   before / will / snowed / tomorrow / wake up / we / it / have / ?
....

5   have / his presents / he / will / opened / his birthday / before / ?
....

6   the students / have / their new teacher / by this afternoon / will / met
....

7   will / by next year / have / they / got married / ?
....

8   Aunt Vicky / you / made / by the time / arrives / have / will / lunch
....

Match.

Eg	I will have read	a	to school for ages by September.
1	Will you have finished	b	their breakfast by nine o'clock?
2	They won't have been	c	each other for three years next month.
3	She'll have seen	d	*four books by Saturday.*
4	Will they have eaten	e	school by this time next year.
5	I won't have left	f	her new boss before she leaves work today.
6	We will have known	g	that book by Sunday evening?

Tick (✓) the correct sentence.

Eg *We will have moved to another city until next year.* ___
    We will have moved to another city by next year. ✓

1 I will have taken all my medicine by the end of today. ___
   I will have took all my medicine by the end of today. ___

2 You will have forgotten me by the time you're thirty? ___
   Will you have forgotten me by the time you're thirty? ___

3 They won't have eaten supper before eight o'clock. ___
   They won't eaten supper before eight o'clock. ___

4 I don't think this programme will have finish by the time I go to bed. ___
   I don't think this programme will have finished by the time I go to bed. ___

5 She will have learnt Spanish by the time she is twenty. ___
   She will have learnt Spanish before the time she is twenty. ___

6 Mum will have dyed her hair before the party on Saturday. ___
   Mum will have dyed her hair at the party on Saturday. ___

Write sentences.

Eg *I'm writing a composition. I'll finish at a quarter to six.*
    By six o'clock ....*I will have written a composition*...................... .

1 I'm learning a new tense. I'll finish at ten to nine.
   By nine o'clock ....

2 They're listening to a CD. They'll finish in half an hour.
   In forty minutes ....

3 She's having a shower. She'll finish at half past seven.
   By eight o'clock ....

4 We're eating supper. We'll finish at half past nine.
   By ten o'clock ....

5 It's raining. It will stop before it gets dark.
   By the time it gets dark ....

6 I'm washing my clothes. I'll finish at seven o'clock.
   By half past seven ....

Write sentences with the Future Perfect.

SIMON'S JOBS FOR TODAY

make my bed
read an English magazine
finish painting my bedroom
wash my black T-shirt
buy a new mobile phone
send all my e-mails
apply for a job
walk five kilometres
bake a cake

Eg *By the end of today, Simon will have made his bed.*

1 ....

2 ....

3 ....

4 ....

5 ....

6 ....

7 ....

8 ....

Find the mistakes and write the sentences correctly.

Eg *What will you had learnt before you go to bed tonight?*
   What will you have learnt before you go to bed tonight?

1 Will you been to the supermarket by two o'clock?
....

2 Will you have learn to drive by the time you're twenty?
....

3 Which countries have you will visited by the time you're thirty?
....

4 She will haven't seen the pyramids before she returns from Egypt.
....

5 They won't has given away all their toys by the time they're thirteen.
....

6 That family will have leaved London before the end of the year.
....

7 Until the end of the year she will have passed her exams.
....

8 David will has finished by ten o'clock.
....

64

Eg   *What will you have will done before you meet me at the weekend?* ....*will*....

1   Do you think the weather it will have got worse before we arrive? ....

2   I will have to lived in this house for thirteen years by next April. ....

3   They won't not have saved a lot of money by the end of the month. ....

4   Will he have and got his degree by the time he's twenty-three? ....

5   Who will have been visited your house by this time next week? ....

6   I think I will have done passed my driving test before I'm twenty-one. ....

7   He will have been finished work by ten o'clock. ....

8   By until tomorrow morning she will have got better. ....

I wonder what I will (Eg) ....*have*........ done before the end of the week. I imagine I (1) .... have eaten quite a lot of food and I will have (2) .... a lot of milk and juice. I will (3) .... slept for at least forty hours (4) .... the end of the week, and (5) .... will have spent about thirty hours in lessons. I will have spoken (6) .... a lot of people and I'll (7) .... watched a lot of programmes on TV. I wonder if I will have improved my English grammar by the end of the week. I hope I (8) .... have learnt some new things and maybe (9) .... some new friends. I think I will have been very busy (10) .... the time the week ends!

Pairwork

Work with a partner. Tell each other as many things as possible that you will have done before you see each other again.

Writing

Write an e-mail to your friend telling them all the things you think you will have done in ten years' time. Think about:

- your home
- your studies/job
- your family
- your relationships
- your holidays and free time

Review 2 (Units 5-8)

1 Choose the correct answer.

Eg Where .... *stay when you're on holiday in Italy?*
a you   **b** are you going to   **c** will you being

1 Do you think David .... give me a lift into town later?
a is going to   **b** will being   **c** will

2 My favourite rock group .... in a concert in London next month.
a performs   **b** is performing   **c** will perform

3 We're not going .... any more time playing computer games!
a wasting   **b** to waste   **c** waste

4 Natasha .... her godparents next weekend.
a is visiting   **b** is going   **c** will to visit

5 What time does your flight .... in the morning?
a is taking off   **b** will take off   **c** take off

6 I'm sure he won't .... in his attempt to beat the world record.
a to fail   **b** be failing   **c** fail

7 .... work until nine o'clock tomorrow evening?
a Is he going to   **b** Will he to   **c** Does he

8 .... we have another ice cream?
a Shall   **b** Will   **c** Having

3 Complete the sentences with the Present Continuous, Present Simple or Future Simple.

Eg They ......*are buying*...... *a new car tomorrow. (buy)*

1 I .... a dinner party at the weekend. Do you want to come? (have)

2 I promise I .... home before it gets dark. (be)

3 He .... his English exam next month. (take)

4 The train from London .... at half past two. (arrive)

5 I know you .... the horror film that's on TV tonight. (enjoy)

6 We .... tomorrow evening. I've already booked a table. (eat out)

7 The plane to Cairo .... at ten o'clock. (take off)

8 I .... that bag for you. It looks heavy. (carry)

2 Find the mistakes and write the sentences correctly.

Eg *I shall keep the pizza warm in the oven?*
Shall I keep the pizza warm in
the oven?

1 Mum and Dad build a garage for their cars next month.
....
....

2 Are you going spend the weekend in the country?
....
....

3 Does this train leaves at five o'clock or six o'clock?
....
....

4 I'll seeing you tomorrow.
....
....

5 Thomas is play in the basketball finals on Saturday.
....
....

6 I'm going to not talk to Laura ever again!
....
....

7 Do you come to the supermarket with me tomorrow morning?
....
....

8 I'm sure it does be hot tomorrow.
....
....

4 Complete the sentences with the Future Continuous or Future Simple.

Eg I ...*will be living*... in my own apartment in London before I'm twenty-one. *(live)*

1 The reporter .... about his visit to China in tonight's documentary. *(talk)*

2 My sister .... when I get home tonight. *(sleep)*

3 I am sure that he .... the race. *(win)*

4 I know it's early but I'm so tired that I think I .... to bed straight away. *(go)*

5 The judge .... his decision about the car thief in two hours. *(make)*

6 I .... to you again! *(never lie)*

7 Our local cinema .... comedy films on Saturday night. *(show)*

8 .... these blue curtains? *(we buy)*

5 Find the extra word and write it in the space.

Eg *I'll will be staying at home all weekend to study English.* ...*will*...

1 Where will you are be working after you're married? ....

2 I'm sure it will be being foggy later this evening. ....

3 I don't know what will be happen if I fail this exam! ....

4 I wonder how much we'll be to paying for clothes in 2030. ....

5 How often will you be visit your parents if you go to live in England? ....

6 Will you miss me when will I go? ....

7 I'll feel be feeling nervous before my exam tomorrow. ....

8 What you will you be thinking about when you wake up in the morning? ....

6 Choose the correct answer.

Eg *Do you think you .... in Oxford when you're thirty years old?*
   a *will be live* **(b)** *will be living* **c** *will to live*

1 I promise I .... you a postcard from Scotland.
   a will send **b** will be sending **c** do send

2 I wonder if it .... tomorrow morning when I wake up.
   a will raining **b** is raining **c** will be raining

3 Who .... for you at the airport when you arrive in America?
   a will wait **b** will be **c** will be waiting

4 What .... this time tomorrow?
   a will you do **b** will you be doing **c** you will be doing

5 .... ever leave England?
   a You will **b** Will you being **c** Will you

6 Who do you think .... the President of America in 2020?
   a will be **b** will **c** will being

7 Will people still .... meat in 2500?
   a eating **b** will eat **c** be eating

8 Who .... your breakfast for you in five years' time?
   a will be making **b** makes **c** will be make

7 Find the mistakes and write the sentences correctly.

Eg *My father is the doctor in Bristol.*
My father is a doctor in Bristol.

1   I've got some relations who live in the Wales.

....

2   What is the name of Prime Minister of Greece?

....

3   I didn't know Smiths were your neighbours.

....

4   Did you stay in a Regency Hotel in Thailand?

....

5   He thinks Ruth has got the beautiful eyes.

....

6   The people should protect the environment we live in.

....

7   My grandfather is at a church at the moment.

....

8   It's one o'clock. Shall we have the lunch?

....

9   The River Thames is in the London.

....

10   Have you seen a dress I bought?

....

8 Choose the correct answer.

Eg *I've read .... good books this summer.*
a *a little*   **(b)** *a lot of*   **c** *a few of*

1   Have you got .... CDs to lend me?
     a a little   **b** a few   **c** a lot

2   We saw .... unusual animals when we went to the zoo.
     a a little of   **b** a few of   **c** a lot of

3   I think we should .... go to the cinema or the bowling alley.
     a neither   **b** both   **c** either

4   We still have .... time left. If we hurry we might catch the train.
     a a little   **b** much   **c** a few

5   There isn't .... cheese on this pizza.
     a many   **b** either   **c** much

6   Are .... the students in your English class as good as you are?
     a either   **b** all   **c** none

7   I don't think we bought .... cola for the party.
     a too   **b** not enough   **c** enough

8   There are .... books on this shelf. It will break.
     a too many   **b** too much   **c** not enough

9 Complete the sentences with **some** or **any**.

Eg *Can I have ....some........ money to go shopping?*

1   We saw .... interesting paintings in the art gallery.

2   I haven't got .... nice clothes to wear to the wedding.

3   Have you got .... time to explain this to me?

4   There's isn't .... milk left so we can't have a milkshake.

5   There are .... great sights to see in London.

6   Are there .... good museums in your town?

7   Would you like .... coffee?

8   I didn't buy .... cat food when I went to the supermarket.

Complete the sentences with the Future Perfect Simple.

Eg   I ....*will not have finished*.... all this homework by eleven o'clock tonight. (not finish)

1   .... you .... your supper before eight o'clock this evening? (eat)

2   He .... to Mum for being rude by the time Dad gets home. (apologise)

3   Those students .... their compositions before the next lesson. (not write)

4   She .... university before her sister finishes high school. (leave)

5   .... your friend .... you an e-mail by this time tomorrow? (send)

6   Do you think it .... by the time we get up in the morning? (snow)

7   I don't believe people .... to live on the moon by the year 2500. (start)

8   I'm sure Susan .... enough food for everyone who's coming to supper this evening. (buy)

Complete the sentences with **by** or **in**.

Eg   Will you be much taller ....*by*...... the time you're twenty?

1   The decorators will have painted the lounge .... the end of today.

2   .... a year's time they will have graduated from university.

3   Will you have learnt how to use your new laptop .... the time we go on holiday?

4   I don't think our guests will have arrived .... eight o'clock as we had arranged.

5   He won't have swum five kilometres .... this afternoon.

6   They'll have returned from town .... an hour.

7   We'll have moved house .... next September.

8   .... half an hour the plane will have taken off.

Find the mistakes and write the sentences correctly.

Eg   *Thousands of people will visited the Acropolis by the end of the summer.*
Thousands of people will have visited the Acropolis by the end of the summer.

1   Will you have washed your hair for the time we go out tonight?
....

2   My mother won't have been done all her jobs by tonight.
....

3   In ten o'clock this evening they'll have listened to ten CDs.
....

4   I think computers they will have changed a lot by the year 2015.
....

5   We will had set off on our journey before the sun rises.
....

6   In the end of October he'll have been in the army for a year.
....

7   How much bread will she have been selling by lunchtime?
....

8   Mum will have go to bed before we get home.
....

69

Can / Could / Be able to & Must / Have to

Can

Affirmative	Negative	Question
I/you can write	I/you cannot (can't) write	Can I/you write?
he/she/it can write	he/she/it cannot (can't) write	Can he/she/it write?
we/you/they can write	we/you/they cannot (can't) write	Can we/you/they write?

Short answers

Yes, I/you can.	No, I/you can't.
Yes, he/she/it can.	No, he/she/it can't.
Yes, we/you/they can.	No, we/you/they can't.

We use *can*:

- to talk about ability in the present.
  She can ride a horse.
  He can't speak Italian.

- to talk about or ask for permission.
  Can I have some more chocolate?
  No, you can't!

- to make requests.
  Can you bring me a glass of water, please?

Notes

Even though we don't use *can* in the Future Simple (we use *will be able to*), when we talk about present decisions concerning future ability, we do use *can*.
We can't finish the job today but we can come back tomorrow morning and finish it.

We use *can* in a negative question when we want to show that we are surprised or upset by something.
Can't you come to my party at the weekend?

1 Complete the sentences with **can** and the words in brackets.

Eg .... French? (you / speak)
Can you speak

1 We .... what he is saying. (not hear)

2 .... some money to go shopping? (I / have)

3 They .... out with us on Saturday because their son is ill. (not come)

4 .... the guitar? (he / play)

5 You .... the cupboard because it is locked. (not open)

6 We .... through those gates – it's not allowed. (not go)

7 .... a cup of coffee, please? (I / have)

8 .... the light on, please? (you / turn)

9 I ....! It's too dark in here. (not see)

10 .... here, please? I want to tell you something. (you / come)

Could

Affirmative	Negative	Question
I/you could write	I/you could not (couldn't) write	Could I/you write?
he/she/it could write	he/she/it could not (couldn't) write	Could he/she/it write?
we/you/they could write	we/you/they could not (couldn't) write	Could we/you/they write?

Short answers

Yes, I/you could.	No, I/you couldn't.
Yes, he/she/it could.	No, he/she/it couldn't.
Yes, we/you/they could.	No, we/you/they couldn't.

We use *could*:

- to talk about past ability.
  He could ride a bike when he was four.

- to ask for permission in the present and future.
  Could I borrow your pen, please?
  Could I take the day off on Monday?

- to make a polite request.
  Could you open the door for me, please?

Notes

We do not use *could* for ability in the past to talk about one specific time when we managed to do something. In this case we must use *was/were able to*.
She was able to post my letter for me yesterday.

2 Write questions.

Eg *use your phone (could)*
Could I use your phone, please?

1 borrow some money (can)
....

2 have a glass of water (could)
....

3 pass me the salt (could)
....

4 use your car tonight (can)
....

5 tell me the time (could)
....

6 use your computer (can)
....

Be Able To

Affirmative	Negative	Question
I am able to write	I am not (I'm not) able to write	Am I able to write?
you are able to write	you are not (aren't) able to write	Are you able to write?
he/she/it is able to write	he/she/it is not (isn't) able to write	Is he/she/it able to write?
we/you/they are able to write	we/you/they are not (aren't) able to write	Are we/you/they able to write?

Short answers

Yes, I am.	No, I'm not.
Yes, you are.	No, you aren't.
Yes, he/she/it is.	No, he/she/it isn't.
Yes, we/you/they are.	No, we/you/they aren't.

Be able to can be used in a number of tenses. It is not used in continuous tenses.

Present Simple - *I am able to, you are able to, etc*
Past Simple - *I was able to, you were able to, etc*
Present Perfect Simple - *I have been able to, you have been able to, etc*
Past Perfect Simple - *I had been able to, you had been able to, etc*
Future Simple - *I will be able to, you will be able to, etc*

We use *be able to*:

■ to talk about ability.
  We are able to see the sea from our house.
  He'll be able to collect the children from school tomorrow.

■ to talk about one specific occasion when we managed (or didn't manage) to do something.
  I was able to help him with his homework last night. (We cannot use could here.)
  I wasn't able to help him with his homework last night. (We can use could here.)

Notes
With verbs of the senses, we use *could* and not *be able to*.
We could hear the thunder in the distance.
She could see that Martin was upset.

---

3 Complete the sentences with the correct form of **be able to** and the words in brackets.

Eg ....*Were you able to guess*............ the answers in yesterday's test? *(you / guess)*

1 .... me with the gardening tomorrow? *(you / help)*

2 He .... maths when he was at school. *(never understand)*

3 .... a motorbike? *(she / ride)*

4 Tom lost his keys yesterday and he .... them yet. *(not find)*

5 .... the situation to the new manager tomorrow? *(you / explain)*

6 Granny .... us on Sunday because she wasn't feeling well. *(not visit)*

7 Angela .... the flute from a very early age. *(play)*

8 I'm sorry, but I .... the children tomorrow. *(not look after)*

4 Choose the correct answer.

Eg (Can you) / Are you able to *bring me my bag, please?*

1 When she was ten, she *was able to / can* speak three languages.

2 As soon as I got home, I *can / could* smell something very nice cooking.

3 Luckily, we *could / were able* to rescue him from the fire.

4 He *wasn't able to / can't* ride the horse and he fell off.

5 *Am I able to / Can I* go out for a minute?

6 Why *you couldn't / can't you* keep your room tidy?

7 She *couldn't / isn't able to* play the piano last year but now she can.

8 I hope I'll *can / be able to* pass all my exams next year.

9 They *can't / weren't able to* speak English when they were three years old.

10 She *could / is able to* drive a car now because she passed her driving test last month.

11 You *can / are be able to* finish your essay tomorrow if you want.

12 The cat was locked in but she *was able to / could* escape through a hole in the window.

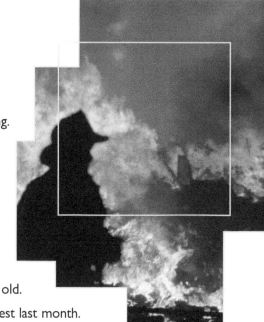

Must / Mustn't

Affirmative	**Negative**	**Question**
I/you must write	I/you must not (mustn't) write	Must I/you write?
he/she/it must write	he/she/it must not (mustn't) write	Must he/she/it write?
we/you/they must write	we/you/they must not (mustn't) write	Must we/you/they write?

Short answers

Yes, I/you must.	No, I/you mustn't.
Yes, he/she/it must.	No, he/she/it mustn't.
Yes, we/you/they must.	No, we/you/they mustn't.

We use *must*:

■ to talk about obligation.
You must follow the diet the doctor gave you.

■ to talk about necessity.
I'm sorry, but we must go now.

Notes
We do not usually use *must* in the question form.

We use *mustn't*:

■ to talk about prohibition.
You mustn't eat in class.

Complete the sentences with **could, couldn't, must** or **mustn't**.

Eg   The fire alarm has gone off. We ....*must*.............. leave.

1   You .... use bad language.

2   Jenny .... find her glasses this morning.

3   Before you get on the plane at the airport you ....
    show your passport.

4   .... you tell me the way to the library, please?

5   You .... say anything about the window we broke.

6   Bob .... never understand physics very well.

7   We .... remember where we had parked the car.

8   They .... give back what they stole immediately!

Have To / Don't Have To

Affirmative	Negative	Question
I/you have to write	I/you do not (don't) have to write	Do I/you have to write?
he/she/it has to write	he/she/it does not (doesn't) have to write	Does he/she/it have to write?
we/you/they have to write	we/you/they do not (don't) have to write	Do we/you/they have to write?

Short answers

Yes, I/you do.	No, I/you don't.
Yes, he/she/it does.	No, he/she/it doesn't.
Yes, we/you/they do.	No, we/you/they don't.

Have to can be used in a number of tenses. We do not usually use it in continuous tenses.

Present Simple - *I have to, you have to,* etc
Past Simple - *I had to, you had to,* etc
Present Perfect Simple - *I have had to, you have had to,* etc
Past Perfect Simple - *I had had to, you had had to,* etc
Future Simple - *I will have to, you will have to,* etc

We use *have to* to talk about obligation.
I have to go to a meeting tomorrow.

We use *don't have to* to talk about something that is not a necessity.
I don't have to finish my homework this evening because it is Saturday tomorrow.

We use the question form to ask if someone is obliged to do something.
Do I have to tidy my bedroom now?
Does he have to take the rubbish out?

6 Complete the sentences with the correct form of **have to**. Use the verbs in the box.

be   do   go   make   pay   take   wear

Eg Sarah ......*has to go*...... to the dentist's.

1 .... I .... the dog out for a walk every morning?
2 You .... the washing-up. I'll do it later.
3 Alan .... his bed. His mother does it for him.
4 .... you .... a uniform when you were in the army?
5 We .... careful when we go on holiday next week. We don't want to get sunburnt.
6 Jeff .... a fine at the police station because he drove up a one-way street.

Must / Have to & Mustn't / Don't Have To

Must usually expresses internal obligation whereas *have to* expresses external obligation.
I must hurry or I'll miss the bus.
I have to tidy my room every day. (Because my mother tells me to.)

Mustn't and *don't have to* have completely different meanings.
You mustn't be late for the concert. (It's forbidden.)
You don't have wear anything special to the party. (You can decide.)

7 Complete the sentences with the correct form of **must, mustn't, have to** or **don't have to** and the verbs in brackets.

Eg You ......*must go*...... and see your doctor about that terrible cough. (go)

1 They .... at the office by 8 am; the boss will be waiting! (be)
2 You .... those magazines out of the library. (take)
3 He .... the cat – I'll feed her later. (feed)
4 People .... litter on the beach. (leave)
5 I .... to buy a present for her birthday. (remember)
6 Those children are lucky; they .... school uniforms. (wear)
7 You .... your food if you aren't hungry. (finish)
8 I .... to the gym today because my trainer said I should have a rest. (go)
9 Mary .... harder to improve her English. (try)
10 We .... on time for dinner or your mother will be furious! (be)

**THINK
ABOUT IT!**

*We also use **must** when we are giving strong advice.*

75

8 Rewrite the sentences using the words given.
Use between two and five words.

Eg *Is it necessary to write down so many words?* **have**
   Do we ....have to write....... down so many words?

1 I couldn't run very fast when I was little. **able**
  I .... very fast when I was little.

2 Talking is not allowed in the exam room. **talk**
  You .... in the exam room.

3 She knows how to play the piano very well. **can**
  She .... the piano very well.

4 It's impossible for them to come and stay next summer. **be**
  They .... come and stay next summer.

5 Is it so difficult for you to sit down quietly and get on with your work? **can't**
  Why .... quietly and get on with your work?

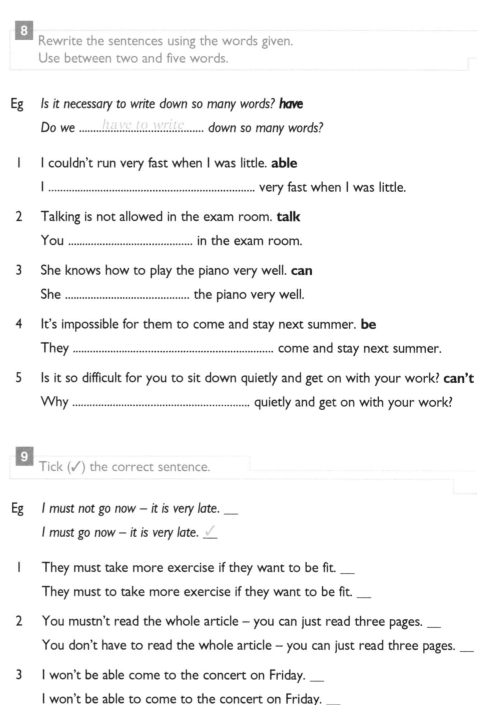

9 Tick (✓) the correct sentence.

Eg *I must not go now – it is very late.* ___
   I must go now – it is very late. ✓

1 They must take more exercise if they want to be fit. ___
  They must to take more exercise if they want to be fit. ___

2 You mustn't read the whole article – you can just read three pages. ___
  You don't have to read the whole article – you can just read three pages. ___

3 I won't be able come to the concert on Friday. ___
  I won't be able to come to the concert on Friday. ___

4 She didn't have to work late last night so she cooked a nice meal. ___
  She didn't had to work late last night so she cooked a nice meal. ___

5 Couldn't you finish your work more quickly so we can go out? ___
  Couldn't you to finish your work more quickly so we can go out? ___

6 He wasn't able to push the car off the road on his own. ___
  He wasn't been able to push the car off the road on his own. ___

7 She can't able to sing but she acts really well. ___
  She can't sing but she acts really well. ___

8 He must to make an appointment with his dentist. ___
  He must make an appointment with his dentist. ___

10 Complete the sentences in your own words.

Eg   *She couldn't* ...... *speak English when she was little but now she can.* ......

1   I mustn't ....

2   You don't have to ....

3   Can you ....

4   Will they be able to ....

5   We have to ....

6   He couldn't ....

Pairwork

Work with a partner. Pretend that you are in control of a space station and that you are making the rules for the small society there. Discuss what ten rules you would make. Use **must, mustn't, have to** and **don't have to**.

Writing

Write an e-mail to a friend, asking them if they can play any musical instruments, do any sports, speak any foreign languages, etc. Tell your friend what you can and can't do and also what you could or couldn't do when you were younger.

```
Internet Explorer

Back   Forward   Stop   Refresh   Home   AutoFill   Print   Mail
Address:

    Dear ........................,

    ..........................................................................................................................
    ..........................................................................................................................
    ..........................................................................................................................
    ..........................................................................................................................
    ..........................................................................................................................
    ..........................................................................................................................
    ..........................................................................................................................
    ..........................................................................................................................
    ..........................................................................................................................
    ..........................................................................................................................
    ..........................................................................................................................
    ..........................................................................................................................
    ..........................................................................................................................

    Love from,

    ........................

100%   Doc: 653K/525K
```

Should / Shouldn't for Advice

Affirmative	Negative	Question
I/you should listen	I/you should not (shouldn't) listen	Should I/you listen?
he/she/it should listen	he/she/it should not (shouldn't) listen	Should he/she/it listen?
we/you/they should listen	we/you/they should not (shouldn't) listen	Should we/you/they listen?

Short answers

Yes, I/you should.	No, I/you shouldn't.
Yes, he/she/it should.	No, he/she/it shouldn't.
Yes, we/you/they should.	No, we/you/they shouldn't.

We use *should*:

- to give advice.
  I should get more exercise.
  You shouldn't eat so many sweets.

- to ask for advice.
  Should we buy her some flowers?
  Should we go and visit him in hospital?

1 Complete the sentences with **should** or **shouldn't**. Use the verbs from the box.

book   clean   eat   spend   stay   revise   take   tell   train   visit   worry

Eg He ....*should visit*.......... his grandparents more often.

1 .... I .... some money out of the bank?
2 We .... out late because of the children.
3 You .... too many biscuits and cakes.
4 .... we .... the neighbours that we're going to have a party?
5 He .... so many hours playing computer games.
6 The team .... harder if they want to win the championship.
7 You .... at the last minute for your test – you'll never remember everything!
8 .... we .... a table at the restaurant for Saturday evening?
9 You .... about her – she'll be fine!
10 He .... his boots – they're filthy!

Ought To / Ought Not To

I ought to start making lunch.
You ought to pay attention in class.
He ought to see his doctor.

You ought not to fight with your brother.
She ought not to watch so much TV.
They ought not to play their music so loud.

Ought to / ought not to mean the same as *should / shouldn't*. We use them to give advice.
I ought to eat more vegetables; they're good for me.
I should eat more vegetables; they're good for me.

Notes
We do not use *ought to* in the question form.

2 Complete the sentences with **ought to** or **ought not to** and a verb you think fits the sentence.

Eg Young children ....*ought not to watch*.......... too much television.

1 You .... that letter today if you want it to get there by Friday.
2 We .... her some flowers for her birthday.
3 They .... the train to go to work instead of going by car.
4 You .... more fish because it is very good for you.
5 She .... so hard – she never relaxes at all.
6 He .... the book again – I don't think he understood it.
7 I .... another piece of cake, but it is really nice!
8 We .... home late tonight.
9 The girls .... their bedroom at the weekend.
10 You .... so much money on jewellery.

3

Write sentences with **should**, **shouldn't**, **ought to** or **ought not to**.

Eg   *wear light clothes at the beach*
      You ought to wear light clothes at the beach.

1   take jewellery to the beach

      ....

      ....

2   wear a sun hat and sunglasses when it's hot

      ....

      ....

3   put plenty of sun cream on if you go in the sun

      ....

      ....

4   eat a lot before you have a swim

      ....

      ....

5   go out of your depth if you can't swim very well

      ....

      ....

6   throw sand when you're playing on the beach

      ....

      ....

Must / Can't for Deduction

We use *must* to say that we are sure something is true.
That must be the postman at the door. (He always comes at this time.)

We use *can't* to say that we are sure something is not true.
That can't be the right phone number. (I've tried ringing it several times.)

4

Write sentences using **must be** or **can't be**.

Eg   *(The phone has just started to ring.)*
      That ....must be....... Sarah – she said she was going to ring this evening.

1   (You don't have your watch.)
    I wonder what time it is? It .... late because the shops are shut.
2   (Your mother said something very critical about your friend, Tom.)
    Surely you .... right! He's always been very kind to me.
3   (Your best friend is flying to England.)
    That .... Martin on the phone. He is flying to England.
4   (You are writing to a penfriend who lives in Canada.)
    What's the weather like there? It .... very cold in winter.
5   (A girl at your school has won a prize for her piano playing.)
    If she won a prize then she .... brilliant at playing the piano!
6   (Your brother has just eaten three doughnuts.)
    That .... a record! Three doughnuts in two minutes!
7   (Your friend is showing you a photo of her mother.)
    That .... your mother! She looks too young!
8   (You have just come out of the cinema.)
    That .... the best film I've seen this year!

5 Rewrite the sentences using the words given. Use between two and five words.

Eg *It would be better for you to go to the doctor's.* **should**
You .... *should go* .... to the doctor's.

1 I'm sure that isn't John. He is in Australia. **can't**
That .... John. He is in Australia.

2 Don't speak to your sister like that! **ought**
You .... to your sister like that!

3 I know he is a thief. I saw him take the money. **must**
He .... a thief. I saw him take the money.

4 Don't read in the dark; it is bad for your eyes. **should**
You .... in the dark; it is bad for your eyes.

5 Fix the brakes on your car or you will have an accident. **to**
You .... the brakes on your car or you will have an accident.

May / Might for Possibility

I might go shopping on Saturday.	You may not like the new teacher.
It may rain tomorrow.	He might not come to work tomorrow.
We might have a picnic this afternoon.	They may not pass their exams.

We use *may* and *might* to say that something is a possibility.

It may rain later on.
We might be late because of the bad weather.

6 Choose the correct answer.

Eg *She .... very clever because she got full marks in the test!*
a *can be*   **b** *must be*   **c** *can't be*

1 You .... be right about her although I'm not absolutely sure.
a should   **b** must   **c** may

2 They .... have too many meals at fast food restaurants.
a may not   **b** shouldn't   **c** ought to

3 I .... listen to you but just this once I will.
a ought not to   **b** should   **c** may

4 It .... rain later – take an umbrella with you.
a should   **b** can't   **c** might

5 She .... be your twin sister, she doesn't look at all like you!
a mustn't   **b** can't   **c** may not

6 You .... to finish your homework before you go out.
a ought   **b** should   **c** must

7 We .... go camping this summer, but I'd prefer a holiday in a hotel.
a should to   **b** ought   **c** might

8 That .... be the best piece of news I've heard for a long time!
a can't   **b** must   **c** should

81

7 Complete the dialogue with the words from the box.

THINK ABOUT IT!

*You can say that you **should** or **shouldn't** do something because it is either good for you or bad for you.*

can't	may	might	must	ought	should (x2)

Mary: Tim (Eg) ......*might*...... have a party on Saturday.
Brian: Yes, we (1) .... to buy him something. It (2) .... be his birthday.
Sue: Yes, I think it is. We (3) .... buy him some snow boots!
Mary: Why? Is he going skiing?
Brian: That (4) .... be right. The weather is not cold enough for snow!
Sue: Well, I heard on the news that it (5) .... snow at the weekend!
Mary: Well anyway, I think we (6) .... buy him something nice, like a warm jumper. What do you think?

8 Complete the text by writing one word in each gap.

Today is a bad day for the Westford family. Everyone is in a bad mood. Why? Well, Dad (Eg) ....*may*........... have to find a new job because his firm doesn't need him any more. Mum (1) .... to go to the dentist's because she has had toothache for two days. Phil (2) .... do a lot of work on his computer but it isn't working properly. Liz's boyfriend has just gone off to America for two years and (3) .... not come back at all so she (4) .... be happy. What (5) .... we do to make them feel better, I wonder?

9 Look at the chart below, tick (✓) the items you agree with and write sentences with **should**, **shouldn't**, **ought to** or **oughtn't to**.

How to live healthily.	
watch a lot of TV	X
go jogging every day	
eat lots of fresh fruit and vegetables	
smoke	
eat lots of fried foods	
drink a lot of fizzy drinks	
drink a lot of water	
exercise three times a week	
go swimming regularly	
eat sweets all day long	
get plenty of sleep	

Eg *You shouldn't/oughtn't to watch a lot of TV because it's bad for your eyes.*
1 ....
2 ....
3 ....
4 ....
5 ....
6 ....
7 ....
8 ....
9 ....
10 ....

82

10 Find the mistakes and write the sentences correctly.

Eg   *You ought to not talk on the phone for so many hours.*
     You ought not to talk on the phone for so many hours.
     ....

1   The door is locked. Daniel should be out.

     ....

2   If you have toothache, you might go to the dentist's.

     ....

3   We might to come and see you on Sunday.

     ....

4   He shouldn't be the new boss. He's too young!

     ....

5   We ought water the plants or they will die.

     ....

6   You should to apologise to him.

     ....

Pairwork

Work with a partner. Talk about what job you may or may not do in the future and how you will train for it.

Writing

It is the summer holidays and you have had a letter from a friend who is bored and has nothing to do. He/she has asked you for some advice about what he/she should do in their spare time. Write back, giving him/her your ideas.

Dear ....,

Thank you for your letter. It was really good to hear from you.
Well, I've got some ideas about how you can spend your spare time.

Firstly, you could ....
....
....

Also, you ought to ....
....
....

It may be a good idea to ....
....
....

Write to me and let me know what you decide to do.

Love from,

....

Conditionals

First Conditional

The first conditional is formed as follows:

If + Present Simple, Future Simple
If she studies, she will pass the exam.

We use the first conditional to talk about something that will probably happen.
If I see Charlotte, I'll tell her your news.
If he isn't well tomorrow, he won't go to work.

Notes
When we ask a question in the first conditional, the *if* clause does not change. The question form appears in the result clause.
If you see her, will you tell her to phone me?
If you get there early, will you phone me?

1 Complete the sentences.

Eg *If I get to work early, ...I will leave early....................* (leave early)

1 If she stops smoking, ... (be more healthy)
2 If it rains, ... (stay at home)
3 If I go on a diet, ... (lose weight)
4 If we get up early, ... (go out for the day)
5 If he gets a job, ... (earn lots of money)
6 If you don't stop hitting me, ... (tell Mum)
7 If he doesn't get enough sleep, ... (become ill)
8 If they learn the song, ... (sing it to us)

Complete the sentences.

Eg   If you ....see................. Jill, will you give her a message? (see)

1   If he .... early, he will be able to meet my parents. (arrive)

2   If she .... too much work, she will come and see us this
     evening. (not have)

3   The weather .... freezing tomorrow if it snows. (be)

4   If you play with those paints, you .... dirty. (get)

5   They won't visit us if you .... too busy. (be)

6   Will you take the medicine if I .... it from the chemist's? (buy)

7   I .... swimming tomorrow if it is cold. (not go)

8   If the food isn't hot, he .... it. (not eat)

9   If the boss .... her work, she will lose her job. (not like)

10   You .... tired tomorrow if you don't go to sleep now. (feel)

Unless

Unless can be used in first conditional sentences. It means *if not*.

Unless you ask your parents first, we won't take you to the concert.
(If you don't ask your parents first, we won't take you to the concert.)

Unless it rains, we'll go for a picnic tomorrow.
(If it doesn't rain, we'll go for a picnic tomorrow.)

Complete the sentences with **unless**. Use the words from the box.

apologise	change her plans	go on a diet	hurry up	pay attention
save some money	train hard	water the plants	wipe his muddy feet

Eg   *Unless you pay attention* ...., *you won't understand the lesson.*

1   ...., he won't get into the team.

2   ...., she won't be back at work next week.

3   ...., I won't ever speak to you again!

4   ...., I won't let him come into this house!

5   ...., you won't lose any weight.

6   ...., they will die.

7   ...., he will miss the plane.

8   ...., we won't be able to afford to go on holiday.

Second Conditional

The second conditional is formed as follows:

If + Past Simple, *would* + infinitive
If they wanted to take part, they would tell us.

We use the second conditional:

- to talk about something which is impossible.
  If I were a millionaire, I would have my own jet aeroplane.

- to talk about something that is possible but unlikely.
  If they asked him, he would probably say no.

- to give advice, usually with the phrase *If I were you, ...*
  If I were you, I'd be more careful about criticising them.

4 Complete the sentences with the Second Conditional.

Eg If we ....*wanted*............ more money, we ....*would ask*............ for it. *(want, ask)*

1 If he .... his work on time, the teacher .... angry. *(not do, be)*

2 We .... very happy if everyone .... all their exams. *(be, pass)*

3 She .... us a cake if we .... her nicely! *(bake, ask)*

4 If I .... you, I .... him what you think. *(be, tell)*

5 If you .... such a lot of work, I .... you out. *(not have, invite)*

6 Your parents .... at you if you .... them the truth. *(not shout, tell)*

7 If I .... to the gym every week, I .... very fit. *(not go, not be)*

8 If it .... so cold, I .... for a walk. *(not be, go)*

9 If the jeans .... cheaper, I .... them. *(be, buy)*

10 They .... if we .... them as soon as we arrived. *(worry, not phone)*

5 Complete the sentences in your own words.

Eg I feel lonely.
    If I were you, ...*I would phone my friends.*............

1 I get bad marks in my exams.
   If I were you, ...

2 I'm always bored.
   If I were you, ...

3 I feel tired all the time.
   If I were you, ...

4 I feel stressed and worried.
   If I were you, ...

5 My friends don't understand me.
   If I were you, ...

6 I haven't got enough money.
   If I were you, ...

Third Conditional

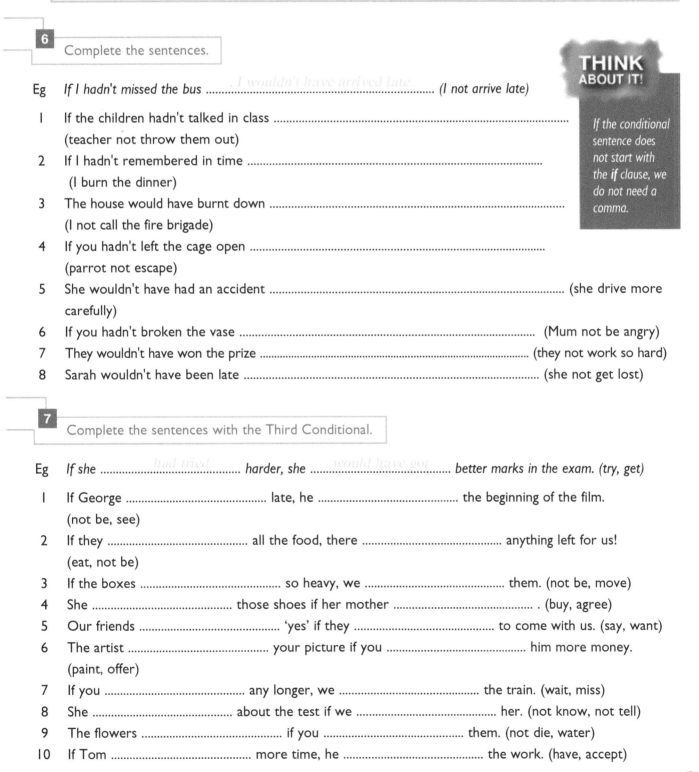

The third conditional is formed as follows:

If + Past Perfect, would + have + past participle
If I had left the party earlier, I would have missed the best part of the evening.
If I hadn't stayed up late last night, I would have got up earlier this morning.

We use the third conditional to talk about something in the past which was a possibility but didn't happen.
If you had come with us, you would have had a nice time.
If he hadn't had an argument with his girlfriend, he would have come to the party.

6 Complete the sentences.

Eg   *If I hadn't missed the bus* ....*I wouldn't have arrived late*.... *(I not arrive late)*

1   If the children hadn't talked in class ....
(teacher not throw them out)

2   If I hadn't remembered in time ....
(I burn the dinner)

3   The house would have burnt down ....
(I not call the fire brigade)

4   If you hadn't left the cage open ....
(parrot not escape)

5   She wouldn't have had an accident .... (she drive more carefully)

6   If you hadn't broken the vase .... (Mum not be angry)

7   They wouldn't have won the prize .... (they not work so hard)

8   Sarah wouldn't have been late .... (she not get lost)

> **THINK ABOUT IT!**
>
> *If the conditional sentence does not start with the **if** clause, we do not need a comma.*

7 Complete the sentences with the Third Conditional.

Eg   *If she* ....*had tried*........ *harder, she* ....*would have got*........ *better marks in the exam. (try, get)*

1   If George .... late, he .... the beginning of the film.
(not be, see)

2   If they .... all the food, there .... anything left for us!
(eat, not be)

3   If the boxes .... so heavy, we .... them. (not be, move)

4   She .... those shoes if her mother .... (buy, agree)

5   Our friends .... 'yes' if they .... to come with us. (say, want)

6   The artist .... your picture if you .... him more money.
(paint, offer)

7   If you .... any longer, we .... the train. (wait, miss)

8   She .... about the test if we .... her. (not know, not tell)

9   The flowers .... if you .... them. (not die, water)

10 If Tom .... more time, he .... the work. (have, accept)

87

Find the extra word and write it in the space.

Eg   *If I were being you, I would go to the doctor's.* ......*being*......

1   If you have had arrived earlier, you would have met my son. ....

2   She will do the shopping if she will has time. ....

3   If you were had done the work on time, you wouldn't have been in trouble. ....

4   Will you tell him the truth if he does asks you? ....

5   If you had listened to the programme, you would find it very interesting. ....

6   They wouldn't have gone on the trip if they had been known how expensive it was. ....

7   They'll build a new house unless if they have enough money. ....

8   If my friends have had more spare time, they would do more sport. ....

9

Choose the correct answer.

Eg   *Unless she reads about all the universities, she* (won't)/ *doesn't* *know which one to choose.*

1   He wouldn't have *be / been* angry if she had told him the truth.

2   Unless the weather *improves / improve*, we won't go out tomorrow.

3   *If / Unless* she leaves now, she'll be in time to catch the last bus.

4   The lunch *will / won't* be ready by one o'clock if you don't start cooking now.

5   If they *wouldn't / hadn't* invited us to stay, we wouldn't have visited them.

6   If you *won / win* a lot of money, would you buy a house by the sea?

7   If your parents *would let / let* you, would you get a dog?

8   If the television *stopped / did stop* working, what would you do?

10

Rewrite the sentences.

Eg   *She wasn't very well yesterday so she didn't go to the party.*
     If she had been well yesterday, ...*she would have gone to the party.*......

1   I haven't got much time so I can't stay any longer.
    If I had more time, I ....

2   He wanted to buy a jeep but it was too expensive.
    If he had had more money, he ....

3   I'll go ice-skating tomorrow unless my sister can't come with me.
    I'll go ice-skating tomorrow if ....

4   She'll go to university if she passes her exams.
    She'll go to university unless ....

5   Her father hadn't read the newspaper because he had been busy.
    Her father would have read the newspaper if ....

6   The doctor said that I should take a few days off work.
    The doctor said, 'If I were you, ...

7   They didn't have any toast for breakfast because she hadn't bought any bread.
    If she hadn't forgotten to buy some bread, ...

8   The students aren't working very hard because they are tired.
    If the students weren't tired, ...

Read the different situations and say what you would do in each.

Eg *If the house was on fire, what would you do?*
I would ring the emergency services / the fire brigade.
....

1   If it snowed hard overnight, what would you do?
....

2   If you saw someone robbing a bank, what would you do?
....

3   If your best friend told your secrets to someone else, what would you do?
....

4   If you wanted to get fit, what would you do?
....

5   If you wanted to get a high mark in a test, what would you do?
....

6   If you missed the last bus home in the evening, what would you do?
....

7   If you didn't get the job you wanted very much, what would you do?
....

8   If you didn't remember a friend's birthday, what would you do?
....

Pairwork

Work with a partner. Take turns to ask and answer questions about what you would do in different situations. For example:

■ What would you do if you saw a huge spider or a cockroach?
■ How would you feel if you were on the top of a very high mountain?
■ What would you do if you saw a rat?

Writing

Write about what you would do in the following situations.
Give reasons for what you write.

If I saw a ghost ....
....
....
....

If I could travel through time ....
....
....
....

Passive Voice

Passive Voice

The passive voice is formed with the verb *to be* and the past participle of the main verb.

- Present Simple: *am/are/is* + past participle
  A lot of paintings are stolen each year.

- Present Continuous: *am/are/is* + *being* + past participle
  The meal is being prepared at the moment.

- Past Simple: *was/were* + past participle
  Our flat was built ten years ago.

- Past Continuous: *was/were* + *being* + past participle
  The visitors were being shown around the factory.

- Present Perfect Simple: *have/has* + *been* + past participle
  The winners have already been chosen.

- Past Perfect Simple: *had* + *been* + past participle
  He had been injured in an accident and was in hospital for a month.

- Future Simple: *will* + *be* + past participle
  The new school will be built just down the road from our house.

- Future Perfect Simple: *will* + *have* + *been* + past participle
  The presents will have been bought by tonight.

- modals (present): *must/can/etc* + *be* + past participle
  The projects must be finished by the end of next week.

We use the passive voice:

- to emphasise the action rather than the person who did it (the agent).
  The new hospital was opened today.

- when we don't know who did the action.
  My car was stolen yesterday.

- when it is easy to understand who did the action.
  The man was arrested last night.

Notes
We don't use the passive voice in the Present Perfect Continuous, the Past Perfect Continuous or the Future Continuous.

1 Complete the sentences using the Passive Voice in the Present Simple or Present Continuous.

Eg   A new airport .... *is being built* .... outside London. (build)

1   All her letters .... on the computer. (write)
2   His car .... at the garage. (repair)
3   The chicken .... at the moment. (cook)
4   Grapes .... in that area of France. (grow)
5   That ice cream .... from natural ingredients. (make)
6   The meetings .... at the moment. (arrange)
7   The students .... by a new teacher this year. (teach)
8   English .... in many countries of the world. (speak)

2 Complete the sentences using the Passive Voice in the Past Simple or Past Continuous. Use the verbs from the box.

drive   eat   interview   make   built   prepare   watch   wear   write

Eg   A new airport .... *was built* .... outside London.

1   Her car .... by her son when the accident happened.
2   The announcement .... in the newspaper.
3   The dress .... by a famous model.
4   The fish .... by the cat.
5   This composition .... by the best student last year.
6   The meal .... while we were talking.
7   This comedy series .... by a lot of people.
8   The star .... by the reporter while they were driving in a limousine.

Passive Voice – Questions and Negatives

The negative is formed by putting the word *not* after the auxiliary verb.
The furniture will not be sold today.

The question is formed by putting the auxiliary verb before the subject.
The furniture will be sold tomorrow.   →   *Will the furniture be sold tomorrow?*

91

3

Write questions.

Eg *The washing is done on Tuesdays.*
   Is the washing done on Tuesdays?

I   The room was being painted.
   ....

2   The cats were fed.
   ....

3   A chocolate cake is being baked.
   ....

4   The lawn was being mown.
   ....

5   Two men were interviewed by the police.
   ....

6   Wine is made from grapes.
   ....

7   All the meals are cooked by the chef.
   ....

8   The seeds are being planted.
   ....

4

Complete the sentences using the Passive Voice in the Past Perfect Simple.

Eg   The apples ....*had been washed*........ before I put them on the table. (wash)

I   The dog .... a bath and his fur was white and clean. (give)
2   The robbers .... before the police arrived. (catch)
3   The lights .... off before we left the house. (not switch)
4   All their things .... into boxes when I got there. (pack)
5   The film .... so I went back the next day. (not develop)
6   The book .... before the film was made. (write)
7   The coffee and toast .... before the guests sat down to breakfast. (make)
8   They .... to such an expensive restaurant before. (not invite)

5

Complete the sentences with the Passive Voice of the modal verb given. Use the verbs from the box.

cancel   deliver   find   finish   give   need   serve   test   touch

Eg   This project ....*must be finished*........ by next week. (must)

I   Her eyes .... every six months. (should)
2   Red wine .... cold. (shouldn't)
3   These extra chairs .... for the party. (might)
4   The parcel .... tomorrow. (could)
5   This electric wire .... by anyone. (mustn't)
6   The meeting .... because of the bad weather. (may)
7   Her books .... in all good bookshops. (can)
8   These pills .... to children. (shouldn't)

6 Write sentences as in the examples.

Eg *the work / not finish / yet.*
    The work hasn't been finished yet.

1 not all the tickets / for the concert / sell / yet

....

....

2 the results / of the exam / announce / tomorrow

....

....

3 the kitchen / already / paint / yellow

....

....

the project / complete / next week
The project will be completed by next week.

4 the house / finish / in the year 2010

....

....

5 lunch / not prepare / until later

....

....

6 the baby / be born / next week

....

....

Changing from Active to Passive

Tense	Active Voice	Passive Voice
Present Simple	*He finishes the work.*	*The work is finished.*
Present Continuous	*He is finishing the work.*	*The work is being finished.*
Past Simple	*He finished the work.*	*The work was finished.*
Past Continuous	*He was finishing the work.*	*The work was being finished.*
Present Perfect Simple	*He has finished the work.*	*The work has been finished.*
Past Perfect Simple	*He had finished the work.*	*The work had been finished.*
Future Simple	*He will finish the work.*	*The work will be finished.*
Future Perfect Simple	*He will have finished the work.*	*The work will have been finished.*
modals (present)	*He must finish the work.*	*The work must be finished.*

We change a sentence from the active to the passive voice in the following way:

■ The object of the active sentence becomes the subject of the passive sentence.

■ We use the verb *to be* in the same tense as the verb in the active sentence.

■ We use the past participle of the main verb in the active sentence.

■ We use the word *by* if we want to say who did the action.

Mum made the chocolate cake. → *The chocolate cake was made by Mum.*

They have eaten the chocolates. → *The chocolates have been eaten.*

Change the following sentences from Active to Passive Voice.

Eg   *They learn the rules off by heart.*
     The rules are learnt off by heart.
....

1   The management is checking her work.

....

2   They took the visitors to the train station.

....

3   They were preparing the students for the exam.

....

4   He has asked his friends to come to the concert.

....

5   Someone had taken their bags to their rooms.

....

6   He will paint the door tomorrow.

....

7   You mustn't leave the computer on.

....

8   He always writes his letters in green ink.

....

9   I can find the books tomorrow.

....

10   You should answer all phone calls immediately.

....

Rewrite the sentences using the words given. Use between two and five words.

Eg   *No one has seen his dog for days.* **been**
     His dog .... *hasn't been seen* .... *for days.*

1   They are servicing his car at the moment. **being**
    His car .... at the moment.

2   My uncle grows wheat on his farm. **is**
    Wheat .... on my uncle's farm.

3   We must clean the house tomorrow. **be**
    The house .... tomorrow.

4   The guide showed us around the castle. **by**
    We were .... the guide.

5   They had eaten all the cakes by the time we got there. **had**
    All the cakes .... by the time we got there.

6   Millions of people all over the world were watching the concert. **was**
    The concert .... millions of people all over the world.

Complete the articles with the Passive Voice in the correct tense.

Several areas of Italy (Eg) ....*were hit*........ (hit) yesterday by bad storms. Many farms (1) .... (flood) and people (2) .... (force) to go up onto the roofs of their houses. They (3) .... (rescue) by firemen and escaped to dry land. The weather (4) .... (expect) to improve at the weekend.

Two men (5) .... (arrest) last night for stealing a television and video from a house. A policeman (6) .... (call) when neighbours heard bangs and crashes coming from the house next door. The two men (7) .... (put) in prison for the night and tomorrow they will go to court.

A police warning (8) .... (give) out on television and radio in the Manchester area yesterday evening when a prisoner escaped from the local prison. People (9) .... (warn) to stay in their houses because it is possible that the criminal may (10) .... (arm).

On Wednesday morning, an SOS signal (11) .... (receive) from a fishing boat that was in difficulty. Fortunately, all the fishermen (12) .... (bring) to shore by a lifeboat and (13) .... (take) to hospital suffering from shock and cold. The men (14) .... (tell) not to go out but they had thought the weather would get better.

Pairwork

Work with a partner. Ask and answer questions using the Passive Voice.
Talk about the things that would be done for you if you won a million pounds.

Writing

Write a short paragraph about **one** of the two processes. Use the Passive Voice.
You can draw pictures or use photos to illustrate your writing.

- choosing players for a school sports team
- making a cake or other food

....
....
....
....
....
....
....

Review 3 (Units 9-12)

1

Complete the sentences with the verbs from the box and the correct form of **can**.

| come | have | help | not cook | not find | not go | not hear | not speak | open | understand |

Eg I ....*can't find*............ anything in this drawer because it's such a mess!

1 You .... to the library now – it's closed.

2 .... I .... a glass of water, please?

3 .... you .... the window, please?

4 I .... French but I
.... it very well.

5 .... you .... to my party on Saturday?

6 He .... but he's quite good at ironing!

7 She .... what the teacher is saying.

8 We .... you, if you like.

2

Complete the sentences with the correct form of **be able to**. Use the Present Simple, Present Perfect Simple, Past Simple and Future Simple.

Eg I'm sorry but I ....*won't be able to come*............ to my piano lesson tomorrow. (not come)

1 The boy .... across the pool so he had a few more lessons. (not swim)

2 They .... us organise the meeting but they want to come. (not help)

3 Dad .... to work for several days because he was ill. (not go)

4 .... him yet? (you / phone)

5 When I was young, I .... the top cupboards in the kitchen. (not reach)

6 They .... us in their car tomorrow because it has broken down. (not take)

7 .... the guitar when you were seven? (you/play)

8 I .... camping with you next summer! (come)

3

Choose the correct answer.

Eg Am I able to / (Could I) have a break for a minute?

1 The door was stuck but finally I *was able to / could* open it and leave the room.

2 He *couldn't / isn't able to* drive last year but now he can.

3 I hope I'll *can / be able to* visit you in London next year.

4 They *can't / weren't able to* help us with our problems but at least they listened to us.

5 He *could / is able to* teach English now because he passed his exams last year.

6 *Could you / Are you able to* bring me a glass of orange juice, please?

7 At the age of five, he *was able to / can* speak two languages.

8 As soon as we got to the restaurant, we *can / could* hear our friends laughing and chatting.

Complete the sentences with **must**, **mustn't**, **have to** or **don't have to** and the words in brackets.

Eg I .....*must remember*..... to take my book back to the library tomorrow. (remember)

1 At some schools, children .... school uniforms; they can wear what they like. (wear)
2 You .... off the bus when it's moving. (jump)
3 I .... to the station to meet him because he is going to take a taxi. (go)
4 We .... our English more so we can speak to the tourists in the summer. (practise)
5 We .... late for lunch because there are other guests as well. (be)
6 She .... so much housework every day – the house is clean anyway! (do)
7 They .... at the airport two hours before their flight leaves. (be)
8 You .... your books lying around on the floor! (leave)

Choose the correct answer.

Eg *She .... be fifty years old – she only looks about thirty!*
  a *mustn't* **b** *can't* **c** *may not*

1 We .... to leave now because it's getting late.
  a ought **b** should **c** must
2 I .... go and see Julie this evening – do you want to come?
  a may **b** can't **c** can
3 They .... be very tired after that long walk!
  a can't **b** must **c** should
4 That .... right! I make the answer £500.
  a can be **b** mustn't be **c** can't be
5 It .... rain later, but you never know with English weather!
  a should **b** must **c** could
6 They .... spend too much money on silly things.
  a may not **b** shouldn't **c** ought to
7 I .... eat any more but the food is so delicious!
  a ought not to **b** should **c** may
8 That .... be the reason for their strange behaviour –
  perhaps we should ask them what is wrong?
  a mustn't **b** can **c** can't

Complete the sentences using the First Conditional.

Eg *They ....won't go....... on the trip if Peter ....is....... still ill. (not go, be)*

1 .... me if I .... you what to do? (you / help, show)
2 I .... to the park tomorrow if you .... with me. (not go, not come)
3 If the fish .... fresh, he .... it. (not be, not eat)
4 If I ...., I know I .... well in the test. (concentrate, do)
5 You .... to get up early in the morning if you .... up late.
  (not manage, stay)
6 If you .... Tom, ... him that I'm expecting him tomorrow? (see, you / tell)
7 I .... late for work if I .... that bus. (be, not catch)
8 If they .... to come on the trip, they .... give in their names now.
  (want, have to)

7 Write sentences using the Second Conditional.

Eg *you / need / advice your parents / give / it to you*
If you needed advice, your parents would give it to you.

1 I / not practise tennis / every day / I / not get / into / the team
....
....

2 it / not be / so late at night / I / study / some more
....
....

3 these shoes / be / my size / I / buy / them
....
....

4 we / have / more time / we / have / more hobbies
....
....

5 I / be / very happy / you / come / to my birthday party
....
....

6 they / buy / a new flat / they / have / more money / ?
....
....

7 they / drive / me to the airport / I / miss my tain
....
....

8 you / lend / me your car / I / promise / to bring it back soon / ?
....
....
....

8 Complete the sentences using the Third Conditional.

Eg *If we hadn't caught the bus, we*
.... the boat.
would have missed
(miss)

1 If my friends had asked me to go too, I .... (refuse)

2 If he had listened to the news, he .... about the accident. (heard)

3 The clothes would have dried out if it .... again. (rain)

4 Alan would have been happy if he .... the exam. (pass)

5 If there hadn't been an emergency, Jane .... the meeting. (not leave)

6 If I hadn't been so tired, I .... so many mistakes. (not make)

7 David wouldn't have met her if he .... to the party. (not go)

8 If I hadn't left the food out of the fridge, it .... (not go off)

9 Write sentences with **unless**.

Eg *I'll see you tomorrow if our plans don't change.*
I'll see you tomorrow unless our plans change.

1 We won't go out at the weekend if the weather is bad.
....
....

2 You won't know what to do if you don't listen.
....
....

3 If you don't buy me some apples, I won't be able to make an apple pie.
....
....

4 You'll never finish your homework if you don't stop watching TV!
....
....

5 If he doesn't train hard, he won't be ready for the race.
....
....

6 If Mum doesn't get back late, we'll go to the cinema.
....
....

7 If her plans don't change, she'll leave for Australia in the summer.
....
....

8 If my friend doesn't like the idea, she won't join in the activity.
....
....

10 Complete the sentences using the Passive Voice. Use the Present Simple, Present Continuous or Past Simple.

Eg The cakes ....*are being baked*.... by Granny. (bake)

1 The members of the team .... yesterday. (choose)
2 .... this house .... by your great-grandfather? (build)
3 The children .... to school by bus every day. (take)
4 .... the baby .... her breakfast at the moment? (give)
5 A lot of oranges .... in Spain. (grow)
6 The flat .... last week. (paint)
7 The tests .... by the teacher right now. (mark)
8 .... these products .... here in the village? (make)

11 Change the sentences from Active to Passive Voice.

Eg We must pick the fruit as soon as it is ready.
    The fruit must be picked as soon as it
    is ready.

1 They make champagne from grapes.
   ....
   ....

2 People can visit the museum every day.
   ....
   ....

3 You shouldn't send breakable goods by post.
   ....
   ....

4 They had ordered all the new furniture.
   ....
   ....

5 They will repair the car tomorrow.
   ....
   ....

6 You mustn't leave the lights on all night.
   ....
   ....

7 By seven o'clock, they had put up the tent.
   ....
   ....

8 While we were talking, they were preparing the meal.
   ....
   ....

12 Rewrite the sentences using the words given. Use between two and five words.

Eg They had eaten all the food by the time we arrived. **been**
    All the food .....*had been eaten*....... by the time we arrived.

1 They celebrated her eighteenth birthday with a big party. **was**
   Her eighteenth birthday .... with a big party.
2 Someone broke into the shop last night. **was**
   The shop .... last night.
3 They are repairing his bike at the moment. **being**
   His bike .... at the moment.
4 The receptionist gave us all the information. **by**
   We were .... the receptionist.

5 My uncle grows potatoes and tomatoes on his farm. **are**
   Potatoes and tomatoes .... on my uncle's farm.
6 We must wash the car tomorrow. **be**
   The car .... tomorrow.
7 I should book the holiday by May. **be**
   The holiday .... by May.
8 We might finish our work in time to go out. **be**
   Our work .... in time to go out.

 Wishes

Wish / If Only + Past Simple

We use *wish / if only* + Past Simple when a situation is different from what we would like.

(I don't have a car.)
I wish / If only I had a car.
(I don't go out very often.)
I wish / If only I went out more often.

When we use the verb *to be*, we always use *were*.
If only I were rich.
He wishes he weren't so late.

We often follow *wish / if only* with *could*.
She wishes she could swim.
If only I could speak Italian.

Notes
Wish and *if only* have the same meaning. *If only* emphasises our desire for a different situation and is not used in the question form.

1 Complete the sentences with the Past Simple.

Eg   *She wishes she ......lived...... in France. (live)*

1   He wishes he .... a sports car. (own)

2   If only they .... go to France. (can)

3   I wish I .... a famous film star. (be)

4   If only he .... more neatly. (write)

5   She wishes she .... more people. (know)

6   Lots of people wish they .... glasses. (not wear)

7   Do you wish you .... in London? (work)

8   I wish I .... chocolate so much! (not like)

Wish / If Only + Past Continuous

We use *wish / if only* with the Past Continuous when we would like to be doing something different from what we are doing.

I wish I was lying on the beach.
If only I wasn't sitting in class.

2 Complete the sentences with the Past Continuous. Use the verbs from the box.

eat   lie   listen   not work   play   read   study   use   ~~wear~~

Eg *Do you wish you ......were wearing...... clothes from the Paris fashion show?*

1 If only we .... ice cream instead of chicken and potatoes!

2 Don't you wish you .... on the beach at the moment?

3 I think those students wish they .... to music and not their teacher!

4 I wish I .... Spanish instead of English!

5 She wishes she .... in a factory on such a lovely day.

6 My dad wishes he .... football right now and not working in his office.

7 We wish we .... brand-new laptops instead of old computers.

8 If only I .... my favourite magazine and not this English grammar book!

3 Write sentences.

Eg *Carly has black hair. (blonde)*
Carly wishes she had blonde hair.

1 Henry is fat. (thin)
....

2 My brother is a student. (rock star)
....

3 The cat is lying on the floor. (sleep on the bed)
....

4 I am bad at maths. (good)
....

5 The football team is playing badly today. (play well)
....

6 My mother has brown eyes. (blue)
....

7 Joe is walking to college. (drive his dad's car)
....

8 Grace doesn't have many friends. (have lots of friends)
....

Wish / If Only + Past Perfect

We use *wish / if only* + Past Perfect to say that we are sorry about a past situation. It shows that we would like the situation to have been different.
(I didn't say good luck to my sister before her exam.)
I wish / If only I had said good luck to my sister before her exam.
(He was rude to his friend's mother.) *He wishes / If only he hadn't been rude to his friend's mother.*

4 Complete the sentences with the Past Perfect.

Eg   I wish I ....*had listened*....... to what the teacher said. *(listen)*

1   I wish I .... some new clothes for the party. (buy)
2   He wishes he .... how to repair computers. (learn)
3   They wish they .... to work on Saturday. (not agree)
4   If only we .... those stupid things to our parents. (not say)
5   Nigel wishes he .... Norma instead of Mary! (marry)
6   Do you wish you .... harder when you were at school? (study)
7   If only I .... to America to find a job. (move)
8   Mum wishes we .... the housework for her. (do)

5 Tick (✓) the correct sentence.

Eg   *I wish it had been sunny yesterday.* ✓
      I wish it have been sunny yesterday. __

1   Dad wishes he hadn't spent so much money on a new laptop. __
     Dad wishes he hasn't spent so much money on a new laptop. __

2   Do you wish you had gone to bed earlier last night? __
     Do you wish you had went to bed earlier last night? __

3   She wishes she had wrote a better essay. __
     She wishes she had written a better essay. __

4   If only I wish I had long, blonde hair! __
     If only I had long, blonde hair! __

5   They wish they had visit London Zoo when they were in England. __
     They wish they had visited London Zoo when they were in England. __

6   If only she hadn't forgotten her mother's birthday. __
     If only she hasn't forgotten her mother's birthday. __

7   They wish it wasn't raining. __
     They wish it hadn't raining. __

8   He wishes he could buy a motorbike. __
     He wishes he could bought a motorbike. __

6 Match.

Eg	If only I had watched		a	their cameras with them.
1	They wish they had brought		b	the tennis club instead of the gym.
2	Do you wish you had dyed		c	more than fifty Euros in the lottery.
3	I'm sure she wishes she had joined		d	*that documentary about the environment.*
4	Those children wish they hadn't eaten		e	late; we wouldn't have missed the start of the concert.
5	If only the bus hadn't arrived		f	so many sweets.
6	He wishes he hadn't driven		g	kinder to their dog; it wouldn't have run away.
7	We wish we had won		h	your hair a different colour?
8	If only they had been		i	through that red traffic light.

Wish / If Only + Would

We use *wish / if only + would* + infinitive:

- to say that we would like something to be different in the future. We use it for actions, not states.
  They wish their parents would let them stay out late.
  He wishes she wouldn't ask so many questions.

- to talk about something someone else does that annoys us.
  I wish you would stop playing loud music!
  She wishes her husband wouldn't eat so much food!

Notes
We cannot use *wish / if only + would* + infinitive when we are talking about our own behaviour.

7 Write sentences.

Eg I / you / dye / your hair (comb)
I wish you wouldn't dye your hair. I wish you would comb your hair.
....
....

1 I / he / criticise / me (praise)
....
....

2 I / my brother / shout at / me (talk to)
....
....

3 I / our cat / catch / mice (ignore)
....
....

4 I / you / run / in the house (walk)
....
....

5 I / David / close / the windows (open)
....
....

Choose the correct answer.

Eg   *I wish you would* (be) */ been nicer to me!*

1   He wishes his dad would *to lend / lend* him the car.
2   I wish you *won't / wouldn't* fight with your brother!
3   If only he would *is / be* more polite to his parents.
4   The English students wish the teacher *wasn't / wouldn't* test their grammar.
5   I wish my friend wouldn't *play / played* tricks on me all the time!
6   I wish you *would / will* come to see me next week.
7   Mum wishes I would *wear / to wear* smarter clothes.
8   I wish you *had / would* come on holiday with me next summer.

9

Rewrite the sentences using the words given. Use between two and five words.

Eg   *I am sorry I forgot to buy you a birthday present.* **hadn't**
       I wish *I hadn't forgotten* to buy you a birthday present.

1   My brother smokes and I don't want him to. **would**
     I wish .... smoke.

2   It's raining and I want to go out to the shops. **was**
     I wish it .... – then I could go to
     the shops.

3   We haven't got a dog but I want one. **wish**
     I .... dog.

4   I wanted to pass the English exam, but I didn't. **passed**
     I .... the English exam.

5   She wants to be tall, but she isn't. **were**
     She .... tall.

6   I really hope Mum buys me a new pair of trainers
     soon. **would**
     I wish .... a new pair
     of trainers soon.

10

Find the extra word and write it in the space.

Eg   *I wish you would to be quiet!* ....*to*.......

1   Do you wish you were being more
     intelligent? ....

2   They wish they had were living in another
     country. ....

3   She wishes she would had saved her money
     to buy a new computer. ....

4   If only the sun it would shine. ....

5   She wishes she had seen her friend win the
     race, but she didn't have. ....

6   Do you wish it would be snow? ....

7   My mum wishes I weren't been so
     lazy. ....

8   I wish if I were writing e-mails instead
     of doing grammar exercises! ....

11 Find the mistakes and write the sentences correctly.

Eg *I wish I am living in a house with a swimming pool.*
I wish I were living in a house with a swimming pool.
....

1 What do you wish you were do now?
....
....

2 I wish you did help me with my homework.
....
....

3 Mum wishes she had taller and thinner.
....
....

4 Do you wish you would here with me now?
....
....

5 They wish they could had go to the party.
....
....

6 If only I hadn't would have lost my purse.
....
....

12 Complete the text by writing one word in each gap.

My friends and I wish (Eg) ....*we*........ had worked harder when we were at school. We (1) .... we had studied different subjects. My best friend (2) .... she had learnt more about computers and some of my other friends wish they (3) .... taken a course in languages. We all (4) .... we had got more qualifications and that we (5) .... working in more interesting jobs. I wish I (6) .... gone to university and got a degree. Sometimes I even wish time (7) .... go backwards – then I could go to school again and work harder! But my mother (8) .... I would stop complaining and find a way to start studying again – she says it's never too late!

Writing

Imagine you are a reporter and you have interviewed a prisoner. He has stolen money from people, he has stolen cars and robbed a bank. Now he is sorry for what he has done. Write your article, telling the readers what Jake wishes he had and hadn't done in the past.

Pairwork

Work with a partner. Talk about things you wish you could change.
Think about:

- things you would change about your life today if you could
- things you wish you had or hadn't done in the past
- things you wish your parents would do

Last week I interviewed a man called Jake. Jake is in prison because he is a thief. But Jake is sorry for what he's done. He wishes ....
....
....
....
....
....
....
....
....
....
....
....
....
....
....

105

Reported Speech – Statements

Direct Speech	Reported Speech
Present Simple *'I live in Madrid,' he said.*	**Past Simple** *He said he lived in Madrid.*
Present Continuous *'I am reading a book,' she said.*	**Past Continuous** *She said she was reading a book.*
Past Simple *'I wrote three e-mails,' said John.*	**Past Perfect Simple** *John said he had written three e-mails.*
Past Continuous *'I was living in London,' he said.*	**Past Perfect Continuous** *He said he had been living in London.*
Present Perfect Simple *'I have lived in France,' said Ann.*	**Past Perfect Simple** *Ann said she had lived in France.*
Present Perfect Continuous *'I've been working for hours,' she said.*	**Past Perfect Continuous** *She said she had been working for hours.*
will *'I will move to the country,' he said.*	**would** *He said he would move to the country.*
can *'I can play the guitar,' said Tim.*	**could** *Tim said he could play the guitar.*
must *'I must go,' he said.*	**had to** *He said he had to go.*

We use reported speech when we tell someone what another person said.
'I am tired,' he said.
He said he was tired.

The tenses change as in the examples in the table on the previous page.
'I saw her at the bank,' he said.
He said he had seen her at the bank.

We also change personal pronouns, possessive adjectives and possessive pronouns.
'I want to borrow your book,' Henry told Sarah.
Henry told Sarah he wanted to borrow her book.

Notes
We can use the word *that* after *He/She said.*
He said he had to feed the dog.
He said that he had to feed the dog.

1 Rewrite the sentences in Reported Speech.

Eg *'I love Michael,' said Tracy.*
Tracy said she loved Michael.

I 'I work in a bank,' said Dave.
....

2 'We are good students,' said Paul and Chris.
....

3 'I'm going to town,' said Mary.
....

4 'I've been waiting for ages,' said Alex.
....

5 'I can write excellent essays!' said Nick.
....

6 'I must buy a new pair of jeans,' said Jamie.
....

7 'I'll see you tomorrow,' said Mike.
....

8 'We arrived late,' said the guests.
....

2 Rewrite the dialogue in Reported Speech.

Eg *Bob: 'I'm going to the supermarket.'*
I Tilly: 'I want to go too because I want some biscuits.'
2 Bob: 'I'll wait for you to get ready.'
3 Tilly: 'We can go to the shoe shop too because I need some trainers.'
4 Bob: 'That's a good idea. I'm going to the newsagent's for my magazine.'
5 Tilly: 'I'll get my purse and then we can go.'

Eg *Bob said he was going to the supermarket.*
I ....
2 ....
3 ....
4 ....
5 ....

3 Complete the sentences.

Eg *Norma said she would help to clean the house.*

'I .... *will help to clean* .... the house,' said Norma.

1 Sue said she had visited lots of countries.

'I .... lots of countries,' said Sue.

2 Leo and Matthew said they were working hard.

'We .... hard,' said Leo and Matthew.

3 Dad said he was very tired.

'I .... tired,' said Dad.

4 Joe said he could repair the computer.

'I .... the computer,' said Joe.

5 Tom said he was making cheese sandwiches for lunch.

'I .... cheese sandwiches for lunch,' said Tom.

6 Angela said she would definitely come to the party.

'I .... to the party,' said Angela.

7 Martha said she had been reading a magazine.

'I .... a magazine,' said Martha.

8 Bob said he could help me with my project.

'I .... with your project,' said Bob.

4 Choose the correct answer.

Eg *He said he .... his grandmother in hospital.*
   a *has visited*   **b** *visited*   **c** *had visited*

1 She said she .... understand English television programmes.

   a can   **b** was   **c** could

2 The girls said that they .... never eaten grapefruit!

   a had   **b** have   **c** did

3 John said he .... meet us outside the museum.

   a will   **b** can   **c** would

4 My mother said she .... make all the food for the party.

   a can   **b** could   **c** has

5 David said he sometimes .... work at the weekends.

   a must   **b** have to   **c** had to

6 They said they .... learning to snowboard.

   a are   **b** were   **c** have

7 Granny said she .... very tired.

   a is   **b** has been   **c** was

8 The manager said Gemma .... good progress.

   a was making   **b** made   **c** makes

Say and Tell

Say and *tell* are the two introductory verbs we usually use with reported speech.

We use the verb *tell* with an object.
He told us she wasn't felling very well.
I told my mother I would be late.

We use the verb *say* without an object.
He said she wasn't feeling very well.
I said I would be late.

5 Complete the sentences with **said** or **told**.

Eg John ....*told*............ me he had passed all his exams.

1 I .... the teacher I hadn't done all my homework.

2 He .... he was going to the gym to do some weightlifting.

3 The teacher .... us she had marked our compositions.

4 Cindy .... she had seen a UFO.

5 The computer technician .... me he couldn't repair my laptop.

6 Martin .... he had read everything William Shakespeare ever wrote.

7 Molly .... her friends that she was having a party.

8 The policeman .... the thief that he was under arrest.

Changes in Time and Place

There are also other changes that take place when we use reported speech.

today	→	that day
tonight	→	that night
tomorrow	→	the following day/the next day
yesterday	→	the day before/the previous day
last year	→	the year before/the previous year
next week	→	the week after/the following week
a month ago	→	a month before/the previous month
now	→	then
at the moment	→	at that moment
here	→	there
this/these	→	that/those

'I saw a great film last night,' said Megan.
Megan said she had seen a great film the night before.

'I left my keys here,' said David.
David said he had left his keys there.

Rewrite the sentences in Reported Speech.

THINK
ABOUT IT!

Don't forget to change tenses, pronouns and *time and place words!*

Eg   *'I want to go now,' said Sally*
     Sally said she wanted to go then.

1   'I can meet you tonight,' said Thomas.

     ....

2   'I'll see you all tomorrow,' said the teacher.

     ....

3   'I saw this film two weeks ago,' said Daisy.

     ....

4   'She will be here at eight o'clock,' said David.

     ....

5   'We're going on holiday next week,' said Jo and Tim.

     ....

6   'I'm eating my breakfast now,' said Carl.

     ....

7   'It is my birthday today,' said Nina.

     ....

8   'I saw Leo yesterday,' said Aunt Edith.

     ....

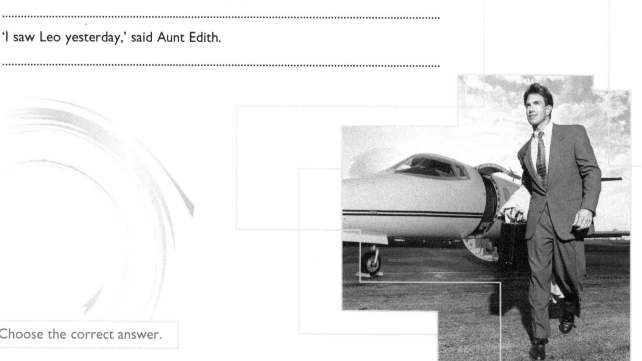

7   Choose the correct answer.

Eg   *Simon said he had been to London on business the month* (before) */ ago.*

1   Charlotte said she might study at Oxford University *the following / the next* year.
2   My brother said he had wanted to stay in bed all day the *previous / before* day.
3   They said they were travelling around the world the *next / following* month.
4   I told Andrew I had lost my purse the day *previous / before*.
5   She said she didn't want anything to eat *then / now*.
6   The teacher told the students to read *this / that* book.
7   Jane said she was happy to be *there / here* when she arrived.
8   Carrie and Jim said they were getting married the *previous / following* year.

8 Complete the sentences.

Eg *Mum said she had made a cake that day.*

'I *have made a cake today*,' *said Mum.*

1 Daniel said he liked the film he had seen the previous day.

'I ....,' said Daniel.

2 Natasha said she wanted to visit the Taj Mahal the following year.

'I ....,' said Natasha.

3 Stuart said he had heard about the accident the day before.

'I ....,' said Stuart.

4 Lucy said she could help me then.

'I ....,' said Lucy.

5 Lisa and Sarah said they were going to the cinema that night.

'We ....,' said Lisa and Sarah.

6 Richard said he had to buy a new suitcase the following week.

'I ....,' said Richard.

9 Complete the sentences with the words from the box.

been	could	couldn't	had	have	lived	living	to	was	will	would

Eg *Our neighbour said that he* ....*had*............ *heard the music from our party the previous evening.*

1 Anna said she .... learning Spanish the following year.

2 I told my teacher I .... understand what she had said.

3 My friend said she was .... in London.

4 They said they .... meet me later that afternoon.

5 He said he didn't know where I ....

6 'I .... come on holiday with you next summer,' said Jenny.

7 Sharon said she had .... waiting for me for ages.

8 Dad said he had .... work late that evening.

9 'We .... been studying for hours,' said Ian and Steve.

10 Sammy said she .... help me do the report.

Find the mistakes and write the sentences correctly.

Eg *She said she will look after the baby while I went out.*
    She said she would look after the baby while I went out.
    ....

I   'I bought your present the previous day,' said Michelle.

    ....

2   Nick said he had forgotten to lock the house yesterday.

    ....

3   Bob said he is driving to work the following day.

    ....

4   They all said the party the before day had been great.

    ....

5   Lynne said she has liked my new hairstyle.

    ....

6   Brian said he must stay in that night.

    ....

Complete the text by writing one word in each gap.

I was talking to my friend on the phone yesterday. He (Eg) ....*told*........... me that he had been on holiday to Italy the (1) .... week. He (2) .... Italy was a very interesting place to visit. He and his family (3) .... walked all round St Mark's Square and they had thrown some money into the fountain. They had also seen the Leaning Tower of Pisa. He said it (4) .... an unusual building and that it (5) .... been smaller than he had expected. We talked about our school work and he (6) .... me that he had (7) .... getting good marks in English. He said his mum was very pleased about that and she had said she (8) .... buy him a new bike if he continued to do so well. Before he hung up he said he (9) .... coming to visit me the (10) .... weekend. We agreed we would go for a pizza in town – that might remind him of his holiday in Italy!

12 Answer the questions in your own words.

Eg *What was the first thing you said this morning?*
I told Mum I was going to have a shower.

1 What has your teacher said to you this lesson?

....

2 What did you say to your best friend yesterday?

....

3 What has the person sitting next to you in your English lesson said to you today?

....

4 What did the last person you spoke to at school yesterday say to you?

....

5 What did your mother/father say to you before you left the house?

....

6 What have you said to your teacher this lesson?

....

Pairwork

Work with a partner. Take turns to talk about things that your parents, brothers, sisters or friends have said to you in the past week.

Writing

Imagine that you have just had a long conversation with your cousin in America. Now the rest of your family want to know what news your cousin had. Tell your family what your cousin said using reported speech.

My cousin .... said that they had moved house. He told me that

....

....

....

....

....

....

....

Reported Speech II

Reported Speech – Wh- Questions

Direct Speech	Reported Speech
Present Simple 'Where are you?' she asked.	Past Simple She asked where I was.
Present Continuous 'Why are you crying?' he asked.	Past Continuous He asked why I was crying.
Past Simple 'Who knocked on the door?' asked Kay.	Past Perfect Simple Kay asked who had knocked on the door.
Past Continuous 'What was he doing?' she asked.	Past Perfect Continuous She asked what he had been doing.
Present Perfect Simple 'Where have they been?' he asked.	Past Perfect Simple He asked where they had been.
Present Perfect Continuous 'How long have you been living here?' she asked.	Past Perfect Continuous She asked how long I had been living there.
will 'When will you tell me?' asked Jim.	would Jim asked when I would tell him.
can 'Which boy can speak English?' he asked.	could He asked which boy could speak English.
must 'Where must you go now?' she asked.	had to She asked me where I had to go then.

In reported speech, questions are introduced by the verb *ask*.
She asked what time it was.

We use the same question word that is in the direct question.
'Why did she come?' he asked.
He asked why she had come.

The verb comes after the subject, as in ordinary statements.
He asked when we were going to tidy our bedrooms.

Notes

The changes in time and place that you learnt in Unit 14 apply to reported questions.

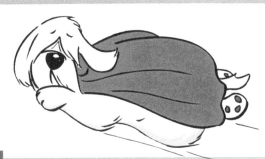

1 Complete the sentences with **said** or **asked**.

Eg   He ....*said*........ he wanted to go to Rome.

1   They .... that they were going on holiday the following day.

2   He .... what I was wearing to the party.

3   My mum .... the teacher why I hadn't got good marks in English.

4   The teacher .... that I hadn't studied hard enough.

5   The policeman .... me where I had been the previous evening.

6   He .... he had bought a present for his girlfriend.

7   She .... him what the present was.

8   I .... my friend how long she was going to be away for.

2 Complete the sentences with the words from the box.

how (x2)	what (x2)	when	where
	which	who	why

Eg   The teacher asked us ......*when*...... we were going to start working harder!

1   The passengers asked the pilot .... time they were going to land.

2   The bus driver asked the young man .... he was going.

3   The receptionist asked me .... room I was staying in.

4   The doctor asked me .... I was.

5   The waiter asked us .... we wanted to eat.

6   The policeman asked him .... he was driving a stolen car!

7   I asked my friend .... she had travelled to France the previous month.

8   The taxi driver asked his passenger .... he was going to meet.

115

Complete the sentences.

Eg 'How are you feeling today?' she asked.
     She asked how ....*I was feeling*.................. that day.

1 'What are you buying in town tomorrow?' she asked.
    She asked what .... in town the following day.

2 'Which is your favourite book?' he asked.
    He asked which ....

3 'Why are you waiting here?' she asked.
    She asked why .... there.

4 'Where do you live?' asked the policeman.
    The policeman asked ....

5 'Who are you meeting this evening?' John asked.
    John asked .... that evening.

6 'When will the lesson be over?' we asked.
    We asked .... over.

7 'How are you getting to work today?' Andrew asked.
    Andrew asked .... that day.

8 'Why are you leaving so early?' Sheryl asked.
    Sheryl asked .... so early.

9 'Where are the keys?' David asked.
    David asked ....

10 'Who have you invited to the party?' she asked.
    She asked .... to the party.

4 Rewrite the sentences in direct speech.

Eg He asked me when I would go out with him.
    'When will you go out with me?' he asked.
    ....

1 The teacher asked what we wanted her to explain.
   ....

2 She asked who had broken the vase.
   ....

3 He asked the coach when the next match was going to take place.
   ....

4 We asked where they were going for their holiday.
   ....

5 Mum asked me who I was meeting in town.
   ....

6 He asked why she didn't want to see him again.
   ....

7 Jenny asked what time I would arrive.
   ....

8 The teacher asked why I hadn't done my homework.
   ....

Reported Speech – Questions

Direct Speech	Reported Speech
Present Simple *'Are you tired?' she asked.*	Past Simple *She asked if/whether I was tired.*
Present Continuous *'Is he watching television?' they asked.*	Past Continuous *They asked if/whether he was watching television.*
Past Simple *'Did Mark give you the money?' he asked.*	Past Perfect Simple *He asked if/whether Mark had given me the money.*
Past Continuous *'Were the children playing?' asked Sue.*	Past Perfect Continuous *Sue asked if/whether the children had been playing.*
Present Perfect Simple *'Have you finished the book?' he asked.*	Past Perfect Simple *He asked if/whether I had finished the book.*
Present Perfect Continuous *'Has he been working all morning?' asked David.*	Past Perfect Continuous *David asked if/whether he had been working all morning.*
will *'Will you help me?' she asked.*	would *She asked if/whether I would help her.*
can *'Can he come out to play?' they asked.*	could *They asked if/whether he could come out to play.*
must *'Must we leave so early?' I asked.*	had to *I asked if/whether we had to leave so early.*

When a direct question does not begin with a question word, we make the reported question with the word *if* or *whether*. The changes in tense and word order are the same.
He asked if she had arrived.
He asked whether she had arrived.

5 Rewrite the sentences with **if/whether** in the correct place.

Eg *She asked us we wanted to visit the London Eye.*
........*She asked us if / whether we wanted to visit the London Eye.*........

1 He asked me I could help him to wash the car.

....

2 They asked us we were going away the following weekend.

....

3 Mum asked me I wanted to watch *Friends* on TV that evening.

....

4 I asked him it was cold outside.

....

5 The teacher asked us we could write an essay about the environment.

....

6 The commentator asked the spectators they were enjoying the race.

....

6 Rewrite the questions in reported speech.

Eg *'Do you live in Cambridge?' I asked him.*
I asked him if he lived in Cambridge.
....

1   'Do you know how to drive a truck?' Bob asked me.
....

2   'Have you been waiting long?' she asked me.
....

3   'Can I borrow your car?' John asked his dad.
....

4   'Was it raining this morning?' I asked.
....

5   'Am I doing well?' I asked the gym instructor.
....

6   'Have you ever been to Scotland?' we asked our teacher.
....

7   'Is it time to go home?' she asked.
....

8   'Are you in pain?' the nurse asked the patient.
....

9   'Did you go to the cinema last night?' Kelly asked me.
....

10 'Will you drive me into town?' Angie asked Tom.
....

Reported Speech – Commands & Requests

Reported commands are usually introduced with the verb *tell* + object + full infinitive.
Mum told me to be quiet.

If the command is negative, we put the word *not* before *to*.
'Don't open the window,' she said.
She told me not to open the window.

Reported requests are usually introduced with the verb *ask* + object + full infinitive.
They asked us to check in on time.

If the request is negative, we put the word *not* before *to*.
'Don't be late,' she said.
She asked them not to be late.

7 Complete the sentences with **told** or **said**.

Eg He ....*told*........ me to wait outside the classroom.

1   The ticket collector .... he wanted to see our train tickets.
2   The ticket collector .... us to show him our tickets.
3   He .... his dad not to be angry about his exam results.
4   They .... it was a boring film.
5   Dad .... me to have my hair cut.
6   The policeman .... the thief not to move.
7   The teacher .... we shouldn't worry about the test.
8   She .... her brother to sit down.

8 Rewrite the sentences with **to** in the correct place.

Eg I told him leave me alone!
I told him to leave me alone.

1   They asked us help them with their English homework.
....
....

2   Dad told our neighbours not make so much noise late at night.
....
....

3   The secretary asked the visitors wait in the reception.
....
....

4   The swimming instructor told us concentrate on our breathing.
....
....

5   The teacher told the students not copy each other's work.
....
....

6   I asked my grandfather tell me about his life when he was young.
....
....

7   I told my mum stop shouting!
....

8   She told them wipe their muddy feet.
....

9 Rewrite the commands and requests in reported speech.

Eg 'Don't eat too much chocolate!' said Mum.
Mum told me not to eat too much chocolate.
....

1   'Open the window, please,' said Danny.
....
....

2   'Stop playing football in your bedroom!' Dad said to us.
....
....

3   'Don't be late home tonight!' Mum said to me.
....
....

4   'Be home by eleven o'clock!' Dad said to Tom.
....
....

5   'Tidy your room!' Mum said to Sarah.
....
....

6   'Please phone me back,' my best friend said to me.
....
....

THINK ABOUT IT!

*We don't use the word **please** when we change direct requests into reported requests.*

Eg *Betty asked me to wash the dishes for her.*
   'Please wash the dishes for me,'
   said Betty.

1 Dad told me not to be so rude.

   ....
   ....

2 The policeman told the boys to stop throwing stones at cars.

   ....
   ....

3 I asked the hotel receptionist to wake me up at seven o'clock.

   ....
   ....

4 My brother asked me to lend him some money.

   ....
   ....

5 My friend told me to hurry up.

   ....
   ....

6 The teacher told us to sit down and wait quietly for her to come back.

   ....
   ....

7 The guard told us not to take photographs of the paintings.

   ....
   ....

8 The students asked the teacher to give them more time to revise.

   ....
   ....

Eg *He asked if had I got tickets for the concert that evening.* __
   He asked if I had got tickets for the concert that evening. ✓

1 He told me to not be so noisy. __
   He told me not to be so noisy. __

2 I told Mum that I am going to buy some new shoes. __
   I told Mum that I was going to buy some new shoes. __

3 They asked why I was waiting for the bus. __
   They said why I was waiting for the bus. __

4 I told my best friend to be careful when she went to London. __
   I told my best friend be careful when you go to London. __

5 The conductor asked the violinists to play more loudly. __
   The conductor asked the violinists that they play more loudly. __

6 Dad asked why had the letters arrived late that morning. __
   Dad asked why the letters had arrived late that morning. __

7 The policeman said the drunken driver to get out of his car. __
   The policeman told the drunken driver to get out of his car. __

8 Mum asked me make the lunch that day. __
   Mum asked me to make the lunch that day. __

Eg *I asked Holly if had she had seen my library books.* *had*

1 The shop assistant told the customer if she couldn't have a refund. ....

2 I asked Lynne do not to bring her boyfriend to my house. ....

3 He asked her please to buy him some bread. ....

4 Frank said he told hadn't been waiting long when I arrived. ....

5 I asked whether Lizzie if she had ever visited London. ....

6 Granny asked me to have visit her the next time I was in the area. ....

7 The basketball trainer asked me whether or not if I had played before. ....

8 I asked Emily whether how long she was going to be in the bathroom. ....

My friend and I went to stay in a hotel in London last month. When we arrived the man at the door (Eg) ....*asked*.......... us if we had already booked a room. We (1) .... him that we had and then he asked us (2) .... go to the reception desk. The receptionist (3) .... us to show her our passports, and then she (4) .... us we had to fill in a form with our names and addresses. She told us we (5) .... staying in room 216 and she said someone (6) .... carry our bags upstairs for us. The man who helped us with our bags was very nice – he told us that there (7) .... lots of interesting sights to see in London and he said we (8) .... buy a tourist map at the reception desk of the hotel if we wanted one. My friend said she (9) .... tired and that she was going to have a shower and lie down. But I told her (10) .... to be so lazy – I said we (11) .... to go straight out and start sight-seeing! She asked me (12) .... I was in such a hurry – but she agreed to come with me in the end. We saw all the sights and we had a great time in London!

Pairwork

Work with a partner. Take turns to ask questions and repeat them using reported speech. For example:

'Where do you live?' ➡ She/He asked where I lived.

Writing

Choose one of the situations from the list below and write a report about what the people said to you, asked you or told you and what your replies were. Use Reported Speech.

- joining a sports club to learn a new sport
- going to a travel agent's to book a holiday with your friend
- going to a university to find out about courses you could take there next year

....

....

....

....

....

....

....

....

....

....

....

Adjectives & Adverbs

Adjective Order

When there are a number of adjectives in a phrase, we put them in the following order:

opinion	size	age	shape	colour	origin	material	noun
beautiful		new		black	Italian		handbag
	large		square	green		glass	fish tank

1 Complete the sentences by putting the adjectives in the correct order.

Eg   Mum uses a ....*big white plastic*............ bag when she goes shopping. (plastic/big/white)

1   The film was a(n) .... movie. (American/boring/old)

2   My best friend is a(n) .... girl. (English/slim/thirteen-year-old)

3   Our teacher is a(n) .... woman. (blonde/attractive/tall)

4   The chairs in our living room are .... armchairs. (large/old/comfortable)

5   His birthday present was a(n) .... T-shirt. (cotton/black/baggy)

6   Our kitchen is fitted with .... furniture. (green and orange/wooden/stylish)

7   They have moved to a(n) .... cottage in France. (stone/old/enormous)

8   She has decorated her jeans with .... beads. (round/small/colourful/Indian)

9   Everybody says he's a(n) .... student. (young/foreign/intelligent)

10 Can you pass me that .... book, please? (green/English/thick)

Verbs with Adjectives

We use adjectives instead of adverbs after some verbs:

▪ be, become, get, seem.

I am exhausted.
He's become lazy.
The baby gets tired in the afternoons.
You seem bored with this exercise!

▪ feel, look, smell, sound, taste.

I feel happy today.
You look excited.
The dinner smells good.
That music sounds terrible!
It tastes wonderful!

2 Complete the sentences with the adjectives from the box.

angry   awful   boring   delicious   disgusting   excited   interesting   pleased   sad

Eg   *He looks .... angry .... about the fact that we broke his CD player.*

1   Mum isn't very .... with me because I didn't do any housework today.

2   The book I'm reading now has become .... – I'm not going to finish it.

3   Charlie the parrot gets really .... when he sees sunflower seeds. He loves them!

4   Her singing sounds .... – just like a cat screeching!

5   Your parents seem really .... I'd like to meet them again soon.

6   This curry you've made tastes .... – you must give me the recipe.

7   Whenever I see Mike he always seems .... I've never seen him smile.

8   I'm not going to eat this cheese. It smells ....!

3 Choose the correct answer.

Eg   *This cake tastes a bit peculiar / peculiarly.*

1   I can't listen to this music. It *listens / sounds* terrible.

2   Are you feeling *please / pleased* with yourself?

3   The roses you bought me smell *lovely / tasty.*

4   You must be *careful / carefully* when you travel on the underground.

5   The film got more *bored / boring* as time went on.

6   She doesn't *seem / be* very impressed with the new teacher.

7   All the students look *tiredly / tired* after their exams last week.

8   We're getting *thirst / thirsty* now – it's time for a drink.

Adverbs of Manner – Regular

Adverbs of manner show us the way in which something is done. They answer the question *how?*.

(How does he drive?) *He drives carefully.*
(How does she sing?) *She sings beautifully.*

We make most adverbs by adding *-ly* to the end of the adjective.
quick → *quickly*
slow → *slowly*

When the adjective ends in *-e*, we take off the *-e* and add *-ly*.
simple → *simply*
gentle → *gently*

When the adjective ends in *-l*, we add *-ly*.
beautiful → *beautifully*
careful → *carefully*

When the adjective ends in a consonant and *-y*, we take off the *-y* and add *-ily*.
easy → *easily*
happy → *happily*

---

4 Complete the sentences with the correct adverb of manner.

Eg *He studied his notes ....carefully.......... for days before the exam. (careful)*

1 She sings ....; I think she should sing in the choir. (beautiful)
2 He behaved .... in front of his friends. (stupid)
3 They shouted .... when they saw Ricky Martin drive past. (excited)
4 The dog ate his bone .... (hungry)
5 I wish you would answer my questions .... (sensible)
6 He always makes decisions .... and I never do. (quick)
7 The cats ran .... round the garden. (wild)
8 He walks .... even though he's got a leg injury. (normal)

THINK ABOUT IT!

Adjectives ending in -e lose the -e and take -ly.

Adverbs of Manner – Irregular

Some adverbs of manner are irregular.

early	→	*early*
fast	→	*fast*
good	→	*well*
hard	→	*hard*
high	→	*high*
late	→	*late*
near	→	*near*

5 Complete the sentences with the adverb form of the adjectives.

Eg *He always does his homework ....carefully...... . (careful)*

1 He speaks .... to everyone he meets. (polite)
2 I played very .... in the school concert. (good)
3 Although he doesn't study ...., he always gets top marks. (hard)
4 He swam .... at the Olympics – that's why he won a medal. (fast)
5 They manage to live very .... because they grow their own fruit and vegetables. (cheap)
6 He can jump really .... – maybe he'll get into the national team! (high)
7 We must arrive at the theatre .... if we want to get good seats. (early)
8 If you behave .... you won't have any friends. (bad)

Adverbs of Degree

We use the words *enough, quite, too* and *very* to show degree.

adjective + *enough* + full infinitive
She isn't old enough to walk home from school alone.

quite + adjective
She's quite young, so her mother collects her from school.

too + adjective + full infinitive
She's too young to walk home from school alone.

very + adjective
She's very young, so she can't walk home from school alone.

Notes
We can use *really* instead of *very*.
She's very young.
She's really young.

6 Choose the correct answer.

Eg   *It's* too / enough *hot in here – I'm going outside.*

1   I'm not clever *quite / enough* to go to university.
2   I don't think you're *quite / very* good-looking.
3   He isn't a racing driver, but he drives *enough / quite* fast.
4   I wish I was pretty *very / enough* to win a beauty contest!
5   She's *too / very* rude to everybody – I don't like her!
6   I'm *quite / too* hungry – I think I'll have a sandwich.
7   I can't wear this jumper – it's *quite / too* big!
8   It is warm *enough / really* to go for a swim today.

7   Write sentences with **enough, quite, too** and **very**.

Eg   *I be / short / reach / the top shelf*
      I am too short to reach the top shelf.
      ....

1   He be / a good / footballer
    ....

2   Donna be / young / go to the disco
    ....

3   It be / hot / go swimming
    ....

4   I be / tired. I am going to bed.
    ....

5   They be / good / but not fantastic
    ....

6   The children not be / old / watch / horror movies
    ....

Adverbs of Place and Time

Adverbs of place answer the question *where?*.
(Where is she going?) *She is going to the park.*
(Where are your parents?) *They are at work.*

Adverbs of time answer the question *when?*.
(When did you see her?) *I saw her yesterday.*
(When will you be home?) *I'll be home later this afternoon.*

Notes
Adverbs of place and time usually go at the end of the sentence.

8 Write the words in the correct order.

Eg   *evening / every / there / works / he*
He works there every evening.
....

1   you / do / day / come / every / here / ?
....

2   at the gym / yesterday / exercised / we
....

3   working / tomorrow / will be / all the students / hard / in class
....

4   laughed / the children / happily / in the playground
....

5   we / the party / last night / leave / had to / early
....

6   in London / this plane / will arrive / in the evening
....

Comparative & Superlative of Adjectives

Adjective	Comparative	Superlative
long	longer	the longest
rich	richer	the richest
nice	nicer	the nicest
large	larger	the largest
big	bigger	the biggest
hot	hotter	the hottest
pretty	prettier	the prettiest
happy	happier	the happiest
intelligent	more intelligent	the most intelligent
beautiful	more beautiful	the most beautiful

We use the comparative when we compare two people or things.
I am older than him.
She is more intelligent than me.

We use the superlative when we compare one person or thing with others.
She is the oldest member of our family.
He is the most intelligent person I know.

Some adjectives are irregular and form their comparative and superlative in a different way to those in the table on the previous page.

good	→	better	→	the best
bad	→	worse	→	the worst
much	→	more	→	the most
little	→	less	→	the least
far	→	farther/further	→	the farthest/furthest

9 Complete the sentences with the comparative or superlative form of the adjectives.

Eg He is .....*the most interesting*..... person I've ever met. (interesting)

1 This is .... book in the library. (boring)

2 Who do you think is .... than your mother? (pretty)

3 Gregory is .... than me when he does his homework. (careful)

4 You're .... boy I've ever seen! (dirty)

5 I think English is .... than German. (easy)

6 My mum is .... than my dad. (healthy)

7 Maths is .... subject I've ever studied. (confusing)

8 I've got .... than ten Euros in my purse. (little)

(Not) As ... As

We use *as ... as* when two people or things are similar in some way.
I am as clever as my sister.
She is as tall as him.

We use *not as ... as* when two people or things are different.
My brother is not as clever as my sister.
I am not as tall as her.

Write sentences using **(not) as … as**.

Eg *my bedroom / nice / yours ✗*
   My bedroom is not as nice as yours.
   ....

I these trainers / expensive / my old ones ✗
   ....

2 my sister / fat / my brother ✗
   ....

3 the supermarket / busy / the bakery ✓
   ....

4 flats in Edinburgh / expensive / flats in London ✗
   ....

5 your brother / naughty / mine ✓
   ....

6 my laptop / good / your computer ✗
   ....

7 their car / fast / as ours ✗
   ....

8 chocolate ice cream / sweet / strawberry ice cream ✓
   ....

Comparison of Adverbs

When an adverb has the same form as the adjective, we usually add *-er* to make the comparative and *-est* to make the superlative.

| early | → | earlier | → | the earliest |
| late | → | later | → | the latest |

When an adverb ends in *-ly*, we use *more* to make the comparative and *most* to make the superlative.

| quickly | → | more quickly | → | the most quickly |
| carefully | → | more carefully | → | the most carefully |

Some adverbs have irregular comparatives and superlatives.

badly	→	worse	→	the worst
far	→	farther/further	→	the farthest/furthest
little	→	less	→	the least
much	→	more	→	the most
well	→	better	→	the best

Notes
We can use *(not) as … as* with adverbs as well as with adjectives.
She cooks as well as her mother does.
He doesn't drive as well as his dad.

Choose the correct answer.

Eg *Dad always eats his dinner .... than Mum.*
   a *slowlier than* **b** *slower than* **c** *more slowly than*

1 Did you arrive at the lesson .... than your friend today?
   a earliest **b** more early **c** earlier

2 Mum doesn't sleep .... as Dad.
   a as good **b** not as well **c** as well

3 Listening to my English teacher is .... than writing compositions!
   a most interesting **b** least interesting **c** more interesting

4 Nobody works .... my mother.
   a as hard as **b** harder as **c** as harder as

5 My friend Jane talks .... than anybody I know.
   a the fastest **b** faster **c** fastest

6 The cats are fighting .... a pair of lions
   a more wildly than **b** wilder than **c** the most wildly of

7 You should eat your food .... or you will get a tummy ache.
   a least quickly **b** less quickly **c** the less quickly

8 He speaks French as .... as he speaks English.
   a badly **b** bad **c** more bad

Pairwork

Work with a partner. Take turns to talk about how well you and
your family/friends can do the activities below. For example:

I can play the guitar better than my best friend.

- play a musical instrument
- speak English
- sing
- dance
- cook
- run

Writing

Write a description of the people in your class using adverbs and adjectives as
much as possible and including comparative and superlative forms. For example:

*My teacher is the oldest person in the class and she can speak English
better than anyone else.*

....
....
....
....
....
....
....
....

1

Complete with the sentences with the Past Simple, Past Continuous or Past Perfect Simple.

Eg I wish I ....*had listened*........ to my teacher more carefully when I was at school. (listen)

1   I wish I .... on a beach instead of learning English right now! (lie)
2   I wish I .... fruit as much as you do. (like)
3   If only I .... a new car before this one broke down. (buy)
4   If only she .... such horrible things to me, we would still be friends. (not say)
5   They wish they .... on holiday today. (be)
6   He wishes he .... in a different place and not in the car factory. (work)
7   I wish I .... play the guitar. (can)
8   We all wish we .... harder for the exam we took this morning! (study)

2

Choose the correct answer.

Eg I wish it .... snowed last night.
    a have   **b** has   **c** had ⊙

1   If only you .... stop doing that!
    a will   **b** would   **c** were
2   He wishes he .... all those chips!
    a ate   **b** wasn't eating   **c** hadn't eaten
3   Don't you sometimes wish you .... taller?
    a were   **b** was   **c** had been
4   Right now he wishes he was ....!
    a am sleeping   **b** sleeping   **c** had been sleeping
5   I wish you .... more to help me in the house!
    a were doing   **b** will do   **c** would do
6   If only you .... me that sooner.
    a will tell   **b** had told   **c** did tell
7   Dad wishes I .... so much television.
    a wouldn't watch   **b** was watching   **c** had watched
8   Do you wish you .... born in another century?
    a was   **b** had   **c** had been

3

Find the mistakes and write the sentences correctly.

Eg Where does he wish he were live at the moment?
    Where does he wish he were living at the moment?..

1   I wish I had been thinner.
    ....

2   Do you ever wish you chosen to learn a different language?
    ....

3   If only you booked the holiday earlier; the hotels wouldn't all be full.
    ....

4   He wishes he hadn't been being so stupid!
    ....

5   I really wish you would be stopping making so much noise!
    ....

6   Dad wishes it will rain so he won't have to water the garden.
    ....

4 Rewrite the sentences in reported speech.

Eg *'I want to visit Egypt next year,' said David.*
David said .....*he wanted to visit Egypt the*.....
.....*following year.*.....

1 'I was sleeping when you rang,' said Jane.
Jane said ....
....

2 'I'll go to the supermarket tomorrow,' said Emily.
Emily said ....
....

3 'We're having chicken for supper this evening,'
said Mum.
Mum said ....
....

4 'I must get a present for my aunt,' said Celia.
Celia said ....
....

5 'I play tennis every Tuesday evening,' said Simon.
Simon said ....
....

6 'I have been working very hard today,'
said Donald.
Donald said ....
....

5 Choose the correct answer.

Eg *Mum* .... *me she was going to be late home from work.*
   a said   **b** told   **c** was saying

1 Dad said he .... help me to move house.
   a would   **b** will   **c** can
2 Hector said he .... watching TV when the earthquake happened.
   a was   **b** had been   **c** would be
3 Maria told me she .... have extra English lessons.
   a has to   **b** had to   **c** was
4 I told Mum I .... to use my savings to buy some new clothes.
   a would   **b** am going   **c** was going
5 My friend said she .... all about computers.
   a knows   **b** knew   **c** was knowing
6 Chris said he .... for me for an hour.
   a was waiting   **b** did wait   **c** had been waiting
7 I told the teacher I .... feeling ill so I couldn't do the test.
   a was   **b** been   **c** were
8 They said they .... visit us in Manchester one day.
   a will   **b** can   **c** would

6 Find the extra word and write it in the space.

Eg *He said he would be help me to find my lost dog.* .....*be*.....

1 Mum told to me that she had a headache. ....
2 My husband told me he had loved me. ....
3 I was surprised when Anna said me she was going on holiday. ....
4 Dan said he had done his homework by nine o'clock the last evening before. ....
5 She said her friend was to coming to collect her from college. ....
6 Our teacher told us that she had been read all our work. ....
7 Georgia said she was had got lost in the centre of New York. ....
8 He said he'd bought his car the previous year ago. ....

131

Eg *'What are you taking on holiday with you?' he asked.*
He asked what I was taking on holiday with me.

1 'When will you be home this evening?' asked her husband.

....

2 'Why do you like university so much?' asked the professor.

....

3 'Are you going out on Saturday?' he asked.

....

4 'Why has she been working so late?' asked Joe.

....

5 'How did you make this cake?' Tracy asked.

....

6 'Can you give me a lift to work?' he asked me.

....

7 'Has she finished her project yet?' Tom asked.

....

8 'Why were you acting so strangely?' asked Nick.

....

8 Choose the correct answer.

Eg *The technician asked .... when my computer had stopped working.*
a I   **b** to me   **c** me

1 I asked the builders .... they were going to be finished by the weekend.
a when   **b** whether   **c** where

2 We asked the policeman where the station ....
a be   **b** is   **c** was

3 My boyfriend asked me if I .... to marry him!
a have wanted   **b** wanted   **c** did want

4 I asked the racing driver if he .... how to drive when he was young.
a has learned   **b** had learned   **c** was learning

5 The doctor asked me .... last eaten anything.
a when I had   **b** when had I   **c** when have I

6 The teacher asked me if I .... alright.
a am feeling   **b** feel   **c** was feeling

7 I asked him .... tell me his name and address.
a whether   **b** if   **c** to

8 Mum told me .... spend too long out in the sun.
a not to   **b** to not   **c** not

Choose the correct answer.

Eg He felt .... when the teacher said he had failed all the exams.
     a sadly   **(b)** sad   **c** saddest

1   He's a(n) .... man.
     a old tall Chinese   **b** tall old Chinese   **c** old Chinese tall
2   You seem .... about the fact that I'm not speaking to him.
     a surprising   **b** surprisingly   **c** surprised
3   The children ran .... up the road.
     a quickly   **b** quickest   **c** quick
4   The baby plays .... with her toys for hours.
     a happy   **b** happily   **c** happly
5   Maybe you didn't read the instructions for your CD player ....
     a carefully enough   **b** enough carefully   **c** more carefully
6   Who do you know who's .... me?
     a more nicer than   **b** nicer as   **c** nicer than
7   I didn't know you could run so ....!
     a faster   **b** fast   **c** fastly
8   Do these jeans look .... the others I've tried on?
     a good as   **b** as good than   **c** as good as

Complete the sentences with the words from the box.

best   better   comfortable   earlier   more   not   simply   the   well

Eg You're the .... *best* .... dancer I've ever met!

1   My car's .... as fast as yours.
2   Is there anyone who plays the guitar .... than you?
3   I think my dog can run .... quickly than yours.
4   That boy behaves .... most politely of all the children in this village.
5   Who else can make lasagna as .... as your mother?
6   Can you explain this to me ....?
7   This is the most .... bed I've ever slept in!
8   I arrived .... than the teacher today.

Find the mistakes and write the sentences correctly.

Eg I do my homework most slowly than my classmates.
     I do my homework more slowly than
     my schoolmates.

1   Mary speaks English the more fluently of all the
     students.

     ....
     ....

2   This is the worse film I've ever seen!

     ....
     ....

3   You don't seem as intelligent than your brother.

     ....
     ....

4   My mum says you should behave nice when you
     are a guest.

     ....
     ....

5   He is too much young to drive a motorbike.

     ....
     ....

7   Dad's has got least clothes than Mum.

     ....
     ....

Relative Clauses

... and that's the swing which I fell off when I was four years old. Look! There's the tree which I carved my name on when I was six!

Hmm - fascinating.

Look, Tonic. I think those are the people whose shop I used to buy my sweets from.

Yes, I see. When are we going home?

Don't tell me! These plates are the ones which you ate your dinner off when you were five ... the table which we're eating at was made by your father ...

pizza

... and this building, which was once a children's nursery school, is where you fell over and hurt your knee when you were five!

Relative Clauses

Relative clauses give us more information about the person, animal or thing we are talking about. Relative clauses begin with a relative pronoun.

We use:

- *who* to talk about people.
  Mrs Williams is the person who teaches English at my college.

- *whose* to say that something belongs to someone.
  He's the man whose house we bought.

- *where* to talk about places.
  This is the hospital where my brother was born.

- *when* to talk about time.
  1985 was the year when my parents first met.

- *which* to talk about animals or things.
  This is the grammar book which I bought last week.
  Where's the cat which chases dogs?

1 Complete the sentences with **who** or **whose**.

Eg *Are you the girl ....who........... lives next to my grandparents?*

1 The doctor .... saw David in hospital yesterday was very helpful.
2 Is that the boy .... father is a doctor?
3 I only know one person .... name is Fabian.
4 Michelangelo was the artist .... painted the ceiling of the Sistine Chapel.
5 Do you know .... wallet this is?
6 Where's the man .... is in charge of this place?
7 That's the woman .... job it is to clean our school.
8 I'm going to visit the boy .... broke his leg at the gym last week.

2 Match.

Eg *I've never met anybody*   a   who got the best marks this term.
1   Is this the student   b   whose work you copied?
2   Shakespeare is a writer   c   *whose hair was as long as yours!*
3   Are they the children   d   who make bread.
4   Malcolm is the student   e   who broke the window?
5   Bakers are people   f   whose plays are still read today.

3 Complete the sentences with **which** or **where**.

Eg *Have you seen the factory ....where........... they make Ferraris?*

1 There's a volcano .... still erupts in Italy.
2 I've visited an island .... rare birds live.
3 He saw a cat .... was as big as a dog.
4 I know a place .... you can buy excellent cakes.
5 A laptop is a computer .... you can carry around with you.
6 Mum's looking for a nice place .... we can go for a picnic.
7 I prefer the trainers .... have got blue laces.
8 This is the first restaurant I've eaten at .... you can
   try the food before you order it.

Choose the correct answer.

Eg *I'm sure that's the hotel* which / where *my parents stayed on their honeymoon.*

1 Have you met the man *whose / who* owns the new fast food restaurant in town?

2 Why did you choose a dress *where / which* doesn't suit you?

3 Do you remember the times *where / when* we were young and we played hide and seek?

4 My best friend is the person *who / whose* advice I listen to the most.

5 I feel sorry for girls *when / whose* fathers are away from home all the time.

6 We had a great time last summer *when / where* we were on holiday.

7 Those are the apartments *where / which* we stayed last time we were here.

8 I know lots of people *which / who* can play the guitar.

5
Join the two sentences.

Eg *That is the boy. He is called George.*
That is the boy who is called George.

1 There's the hotel. We stayed there last month.
....

2 Who was the Greek poet? He wrote *The Iliad*.
....

3 I've got a great English teacher. Her name is Mrs Henderson.
....

4 It was very hot one year. We were in Venice then.
....

5 We've got a new puppy. It's learning to walk on a lead.
....

6 This is the woman. She can speak six languages.
....

7 They live in a big house. It has got a beautiful garden.
....

8 Can you see the mountain? It is the highest on the island.
....

Defining Relative Clauses

We use defining relative clauses to give essential information about the animal, person or thing we are talking about. Without the information in a defining relative clause, the sentence would not make sense. We do not use commas in this type of clause.

She's the girl who has a degree in ancient history.
We stayed in a hotel which was built out of marble.
He's the man whose wife has won the lottery.

Notes
In defining relative clauses, we can use *that* instead of *who* and *which*.
There's the house which my uncle built.
There's the house that my uncle built.

We do not need to use the relative pronouns *who, which* and *that* when they are the object of the defining relative clause.
Here's the shoe shop which Kim likes.
Here's the shoe shop Kim likes.

6 Choose the correct answer.

Eg   *That's the ladder .... Paul fell off yesterday.*
    a where   **b** what   **c** which

1   Where's the man .... has lost his car keys?
    a what   **b** whose   **c** who

2   I'm wearing the bracelet .... you bought me for my birthday.
    a when   **b** −   **c** who

3   Where are the photos .... you took last weekend?
    a that   **b** when   **c** where

4   She's the girl .... David wants to marry.
    a whose   **b** what   **c** who

5   I've met a man .... brother is a famous actor.
    a who   **b** −   **c** whose

6   John's been promoted to manager at the office .... he works.
    a −   **b** where   **c** which

7   This is the place I .... was telling you about.
    a −   **b** what   **c** where

8   Where are the keys .... open the garage door?
    a who   **b** which   **c** what

7 Match.

Eg   The hotel which burnt down last spring   a   that tells us what words mean.
1   The airport where we're landing   b   who can repair computers?
2   Do you know anybody   c   is my brother.
3   The young man who's got a moustache   d   *has been rebuilt.*
4   A dictionary is a book   e   who robbed the local bank.
5   The Pyramids were built by people   f   hasn't got many shops.
6   The police have caught the man   g   who lived a very long time ago.

137

Non-Defining Relative Clauses

We use non-defining relative clauses to give extra information about the person, animal or thing we are talking about. This information is not essential to the meaning of the sentence. Non-defining relative clauses are separated from the main sentence by commas.
My Mum's best friend, who is a nurse, lives next door to us.
London, which is the capital of England, is a fascinating city.

Notes

We cannot leave the relative pronoun out of a non-defining relative clause.
My red jacket, which I bought in the sales last year, is too small for me now.

We cannot use *that* instead of *who* or *which* in a non-defining relative clause.
The City Hotel, which has got two hundred rooms, opened last week.

8 Write **D** for Defining Relative Clause and **N** for Non-Defining Relative Clause.

Eg   *I know a family who travel round the country in a caravan.* ...*D*...

I   I found the keys which you left on your desk. ....

2   I really like my friend's dog, whose name is Misty. ....

3   Do you remember the place where we went for our first holiday? ....

4   Buckingham Palace, which is the home of the Queen of England, is a popular tourist attraction. ....

5   Have you still got the ring that I gave you for your birthday? ....

6   Robbie Williams, who once gave me his autograph, is a great singer. ....

7   I think that's the man whose dog bit my friend. ....

8   I've just read a book about Neil Armstrong, who was the first man to walk on the moon. ....

9   Isn't 1995 the year when we went on holiday to Holland? ....

10   The boys at the back of the class, who are making a noise, are always getting into trouble. ....

9 Add commas where necessary.

Eg *Our neighbour who looks like Brad Pitt has got a new dog.*

1 J K Rowling is the author whose books are read in many countries.

2 The Natural History Museum in London where there is a model of a dinosaur is a good place to take children.

3 *The Sunflowers* was painted by an artist whose name was Vincent Van Gogh.

4 My best friend who works at the university is getting married next month.

5 My father's mother who lived to be ninety-nine was only 1.40 metres tall.

6 People who have to watch their weight shouldn't eat a lot of cakes.

7 There was a huge traffic jam when we decided to travel into town yesterday.

8 George is the boy in the photograph holding the kitten which he got as a present.

9 This restaurant opened last month when I was on holiday.

10 My school which is 100 years old was knocked down in September.

10 Complete the sentences with relative clauses from the list.

Eg *that shows us where the countries of the world are*

a when life was hard for many people
b where many people go to find cures for illnesses
c which are on top of each other
d which is practised in many eastern countries
e who collect stamps
f who make clocks and watches
g who writes songs about life in America
h whose films are very popular

Eg *An atlas is a book that shows us where the countries of the world are* ....

1 Bunk beds are beds ....

2 Bruce Springsteen is a rock singer ....

3 Horologists are people ....

4 Philatelists are people ....

5 Buddhism is a religion ....

6 Lourdes is a place ....

7 The nineteenth century was a time ....

8 Julia Roberts is an actress ....

Tick (✓) the correct sentence.

Eg *Kate Winslet is the actress which starred in* Titanic. __
    Kate Winslet is the actress who starred in Titanic. ✓

1 MP3 players, which are becoming very popular, are still expensive. __
   MP3 players which are becoming popular are still expensive. __
2 I'm really glad I've got a friend who mends computers. __
   I'm really glad I've got a friend, who mends computers. __
3 In the nineteenth century, where Victoria was Queen of England, people worked hard. __
   In the nineteenth century, when Victoria was Queen of England, people worked hard. __
4 The Mediterranean diet, what includes a lot of olive oil, is very healthy. __
   The Mediterranean diet, which includes a lot of olive oil, is very healthy. __
5 Bill Clinton is the man that was President of the United States in 1998. __
   Bill Clinton is the man who he was President of the United States in 1998. __
6 Loch Ness is the place in Scotland which people say they have seen a monster. __
   Loch Ness is the place in Scotland where people say they have seen a monster. __

12

Complete the text by writing one word in each gap.

I went out yesterday with my fiancé Mark. He's the man (Eg) ....*who*........ I'm going to marry next year.
We went to a town (1) .... is called Hilltown, not far from where we live. The first shop we
went to was the place (2) .... they make special jewellery. We want to find a wedding ring
(3) .... is very unusual. I'd like a ring made out of Welsh gold, but the man (4) ....
owns that particular shop said he didn't have any rings like that. He told us he has a colleague
(5) .... daughter has got a Welsh gold ring and he said he would find out (6) ....
she got it from and let us know. After we'd done a bit of shopping, we went to visit Mark's grandmother
(7) .... lives near Hilltown. Her flat, (8) .... is small but very nice, is next to the
park (9) .... Mark and I first met, so it's always nice to go there. At half past eight,
(10) .... we realised how late it was, we said goodbye to Mark's grandmother and left for
home. We stopped for a pizza at the café (11) .... is owned by Mark's cousin, and when we
arrived home at ten o'clock, Mark's mum, (12) .... had prepared a meal for us, said she had
been wondering where we were!

13

Find the extra word and write it in the space.

Eg *Isn't that the hotel where your mum works there?* ....*there*....

1 Our neighbours, who they don't like animals, throw stones at our dog. ....
2 This is the book which who I've been reading for the last three weeks. ....
3 The hospital in where I was born has been knocked down. ....
4 Chocolate, which is my favourite food, that is fattening if you eat a lot of it. ....
5 My friend Louise, whose dress which I've borrowed, is exactly the same height as me. ....
6 What's the name of that rock group whose CDs which your brother listens to all the time? ....
7 Where is the kitten what which you found? ....
8 Fruit and vegetables, which they contain lots of vitamins, are good for your skin. ....

14 Complete the sentences with a relative clause and your own ideas.

Eg *Athens is a city* 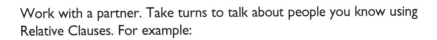 ....

1 My mother is a person ....

2 I know a man ....

3 Italy is a country ....

4 I've seen a dog ....

5 My computer is a thing ....

6 I don't know anybody ....

Pairwork

Work with a partner. Take turns to talk about people you know using Relative Clauses. For example:

Mrs Thomson is the woman who lives next door to my grandmother.
Andrew is the man whose house is behind mine.

Writing

Write an e-mail to your penfriend in England telling them about the town where you live. Think about:

- the buildings (where they are, what they are for)
- the shops (what you can buy there, who owns them)
- people (who they are, what they do, where they live)
- any other things in your town that you think are interesting

---

Internet Explorer

| Back | Forward | Stop | Refresh | Home | AutoFill | Print | Mail |

Address:

Dear ....,

....

....

....

....

....

....

....

....

Lots of love,

....

100%   Doc: 653K/525K

Gerunds and Infinitives

I can't help looking good in whatever I wear.

Maybe you should try to find something ... umm ... less colourful.

I think I'll start wearing more unusual clothes.

I can't imagine going out with you dressed like that!

No, I'm definitely not used to seeing you dressed like that!

Let's stop looking for new clothes for you and start shopping for some nice jewellery for me!

But I can't afford to buy nice jewellery!

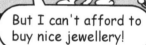

Gerunds

Gerunds are verbs with the *-ing* ending.
studying
dancing
learning

We use gerunds:

■ as nouns.
They love walking.
I hate running.
My brother enjoys building.

■ as the subject of a sentence.
Sailing is my favourite hobby.
Studying is not something I enjoy.

■ after prepositions.
I'm not good at skiing.
We're looking forward to seeing you soon.

■ after the verb *go* when we are talking about sports.
I hope we go snowboarding this winter.

■ after some verbs and phrases.

admit
be used to
deny
can't help
can't stand
dislike
(don't) mind
enjoy
feel like
finish
hate
imagine
keep
like
love
miss
practise
spend time

I don't mind doing the washing-up.
Keep walking in that direction.
They love swimming in the sea.

1 Complete the sentences using Gerunds.

Eg I enjoy ....*writing*............ e-mails to people who live in other countries. (write)

1 Molly's really good at .... new languages. (learn)
2 .... for the Olympics is extremely hard work. (train)
3 Thanks for .... me to clean the car. (help)
4 I love .... breakfast for my family at the weekends. (make)
5 I've just read an interesting book about .... your brain! (exercise)
6 I'm interested in .... a job in London. (get)
7 My friend hates .... a lot of money on clothes. (spend)
8 If you go .... later, I want to come too. (swim)
9 There's no point in .... him what to do. He never listens! (tell)
10 .... too much sugar is not good for you. (eat)

2 Write sentences.

Eg He / enjoy / fish / in the lake
    He enjoys fishing in the lake.

1 My father / hate / go / to work / early
   ....

2 I / enjoy / meet / new people
   ....

3 She / not mind / get up / early
   ....

4 You / spend / hours / listen / to CDs / ?
   ....

5 How often / do you go / ski / ?
   ....

6 I / enjoy / receive / postcards
   ....

7 They / be used to / eat / spicy food
   ....

8 We / not feel like / go out / tonight
   ....

3 Complete the sentences with Gerunds. Use the verbs from the box.

do	eat	go	hit	help	laugh	listen	live	play	speak	steal

Eg I can't imagine ....*living*............ in America.

1 My sister can't stand .... mushrooms.
2 I feel like .... to watch a football match.
3 If you don't practise .... English, you won't pass your oral exam.
4 Most people enjoy .... to music.
5 The thief admitted .... the money but denied .... the old man.
6 I don't mind .... you with your English homework, but I can't stand .... your maths with you!
7 He tells such funny jokes that I can't help .... when I talk to him.
8 She should practise .... the piano every day if she wants to become a professional musician.

Infinitives after Verbs

We make infinitives by adding *to* to the verb.
to see
to wonder
to search

Some verbs are followed by the infinitive:

afford
allow
arrange
ask
decide
hope
invite
learn
manage
need
offer
persuade
plan
promise
refuse
want
would like

I'm allowed to stay out until midnight on Saturdays.
He needs to see a doctor.
We persuaded her to tell the truth.

4 Write sentences with Infinitives. Use the verbs from the box.

| buy | give | learn | leave | meet | take | tidy | visit | win |

Eg *he / would like / India*
He would like to visit India.

1 Frank / want / me / a newspaper / at the newsagent's
   ....
   ....

2 I / decide / Spanish / last year
   ....
   ....

3 Mum / refuse / my room
   ....
   ....

4 the teacher / promise / me / extra lessons
   ....
   ....

5 I / plan / home / when I'm twenty-one
   ....
   ....

6 they / hope / the lottery
   ....
   ....

7 we / arrange / outside the cinema / at eight o'clock
   ....
   ....

8 Lily / ask / Vicky / the children / to school
   ....
   ....

Infinitives after Adjectives

Some adjectives are followed by the infinitive:

amazed
fascinated
glad
happy
sad
sorry
surprised
wonderful

I'm happy to hear that you got the job.
She was glad to be chosen for the team.
It's wonderful to be here.

Notes
We use the infinitive with the words *too* and *enough*.
It's too hot to go out for a walk.
It's not cool enough to go out for a walk.

5 Complete the sentences with the words from the box.

| enough | happy | lazy | sad | surprised | to (x2) | too | wonderful |

Eg   I'm ....*happy*............ to say that you have passed all your exams.

1   She's .... tired to work.
2   We were .... to hear the amazing news.
3   The fridge isn't cold .... to keep the ice cream in.
4   I was sorry .... hear that you have been ill.
5   Is he clever enough .... understand the physics lesson?
6   It was .... to see our grandchildren after such a long time.
7   All the children were very .... to hear that their grandmother had died.
8   He's too .... to do any work.

6 Choose the correct answer.

Eg   *I've just finished* to write / (writing) *a letter to my godmother.*

1   His parents persuaded Thomas *not to leave / not leaving* school.
2   He keeps *to tell / telling* me he loves me.
3   Can you manage *to get / getting* the afternoon off tomorrow?
4   How did you learn *doing / to do* such good card tricks?
5   I don't feel like *to eat / eating* out tonight.
6   Why don't we offer *to help / helping* Dad do the gardening?
7   He decided *to move / moving* to America to look for work.
8   Do you miss *seeing / to see* your parents every day now that you've moved into your own flat?

145

Complete the sentences with Gerunds or Infinitives.

Eg   I enjoy ....*playing*........................ computer games with my sons. (play)

1   We don't want .... anything today except lie on the beach! (do)

2   Our visitors aren't used to .... so much bread with their meals. (eat)

3   Can you imagine .... a ghost? (see)

4   She promised .... politely when she went to stay with her aunt. (behave)

5   I wish I could afford .... on holiday to Australia. (go)

6   Mum can't stand .... people be cruel to dogs and cats. (see)

7   What do you hope .... when you're older? (be)

8   I want to spend some time .... this summer. (relax)

Gerund or Infinitive?

Some verbs can be followed by the gerund or the infinitive without a change in meaning:

- begin, continue, hate, like, start.

    They began working at nine o'clock.
    They began to work at nine o'clock.

    The footballers continued playing.
    The footballers continued to play.

    We hate travelling by bus.
    We hate to travel by bus.

    I like walking in the rain.
    I like to walk in the rain.

    The choir started to sing.
    The choir started singing.

Some other verbs can also be followed by the gerund or the infinitive, but there is a change in meaning:

- forget, go on, regret, remember, stop, try.

    I forgot to go to the meeting. (I didn't remember, so I didn't go.)
    I forget being at that meeting. (I have no memory of being at the meeting.)

    The speaker went on to talk about other subjects. (The speaker changed the topic of his talk.)
    The speaker went on talking for two hours. (The speaker spoke about the same topic.)

    I regret to tell you that your cat was killed on the road. (I'm sorry to give this news.)
    I regret telling you my secret because you told everyone else. (I wish I hadn't told you.)

    I remembered to lock the door this morning. (I didn't forget.)
    I think I remember locking the door this morning but I'm not sure. (I have the memory of it.)

    They stopped to get some petrol. (They stopped one unmentioned activity, eg driving, to get petrol.)
    They stopped driving. (They stopped the mentioned activity.)

    Try adding salt to the soup if it is tasteless. (Adding salt might make the soup taste better.)
    Try to take the egg out of the frying pan without breaking it. (You may not be able to do it, but you should try to do it.)

8 Complete the sentences with the verbs from the box in the correct form.

continue   go on   hate   like   regret   remember   start   try (x2)

Eg It ....*started*............. to rain at seven this morning.

1 Have you ever .... to understand Japanese?

2 I can't .... studying all night!

3 They .... to leave their dog alone when they go out for the day.

4 Did you .... to close all the windows before you left the house?

5 I .... saying those awful things to my friend.

6 Do you .... eating Chinese food?

7 If you can't get a good picture on the television, ... moving the aerial round.

8 The students .... working after the break.

9 Tick (✓) the correct sentence.

Eg I can remember to go on holiday to France when I was five. _____
    I can remember going on holiday to France when I was five. ___✓___

1 I stopped to talk and started listening to the teacher. _____
   I stopped talking and started listening to the teacher. _____

2 I enjoy watching television at the weekends. _____
   I enjoy to watch television at the weekends. _____

3 Jim took the job in 2001 and soon went on becoming a senior manager. _____
   Jim took the job in 2001 and soon went on to become a senior manager. _____

4 I don't remember to say you were ugly! _____
   I don't remember saying you were ugly! _____

5 Did he deny to take the car? _____
   Did he deny taking the car? _____

6 I'd like to see the Pyramids. _____
   I'd like seeing the Pyramids. _____

7 I forgot to post the letters! _____
   I forgot posting the letters! _____

8 We regret telling you that you did not get the job. _____
   We regret to tell you that you did not get the job. _____

10 Find the mistakes and write the sentences correctly.

Eg *I don't remember to lock the door this morning.*
I don't remember locking the door this morning.
....

1 It's lovely to seeing you again so soon.

....

2 I offered going with him to the dentist, but he said 'no'.

....

3 Mum can't afford buy herself a new car at the moment.

....

4 They stopped to talk when the teacher came in.

....

5 I need practising writing compositions so I can pass my English exam.

....

6 We've arranged meeting at nine o'clock in the library.

....

11 Complete the text by writing one word in each gap.

I had a wonderful time last weekend. I had wanted (Eg) ....*to*............ stay at my friend's house for ages, and my mum finally said I was (1) .... to go. When I arrived we felt (2) .... having something to eat. My friend can't (3) .... meat and I hate vegetables, so it was a while before we decided what (4) .... have! In the end we agreed to (5) .... spaghetti with a cheese sauce. My friend had arranged for us to (6) .... to the ice rink in the afternoon. She'd promised to (7) .... me how to skate. I loved it – even though I couldn't (8) .... falling over all the time! I can't imagine ever being good (9) .... ice skating. In the evening we had planned to (10) .... a nice meal for my friend's mum and dad, so we had to start searching for recipes again! Anyway, we managed to (11) .... a nice recipe and we all enjoyed our dinner together. I'd forgotten to take a good book to read in bed, but my friend lent me one of her books, which was great because I'm not (12) .... to going to sleep without (13) .... in bed first. I had a really brilliant weekend, and when it was time for me to go, we promised (14) .... see each other again very soon.

12 Complete the sentences using gerunds or infinitives and your own words.

Eg   *When I'm older, I hope* ....*to buy a cottage in the country.*..

1   I think I will continue ....

2   My mum promised ....

3   I'm not used to ....

4   I like to spend time ....

5   I'm not strong enough ....

6   I need ....

7   I'm too lazy ....

8   I'm going to ask the teacher ....

Pairwork

Work with a partner. Take turns to ask and answer questions using verbs from this unit. Use the gerund and the infinitive. For example:

What can't you stand doing on Saturdays?
What have you refused to do this week?
What do you dislike eating the most?

Writing

Write a report for your English teacher about what you did last weekend. Remember to say what you liked, didn't like, enjoyed, hated, etc, as well as saying something about your general likes and dislikes. Use as many gerunds and infinitives as you can.

....
....
....
....
....
....
....
....
....
....

Causative

Causative

Tense	Example
Present Simple	*I have my car washed every month.*
Present Continuous	*She is having her hair cut at the moment.*
Past Simple	*We had our house repainted last year.*
Past Continuous	*They were having their washing machine repaired.*
Present Perfect Simple	*We have had the windows cleaned.*
Present Perfect Continuous	*We have been having the house decorated.*
Past Perfect Simple	*He had already had his bike repaired.*
Past Perfect Continuous	*She had been having her dress designed.*
Future Simple	*I'll have my hair dyed blond!*
Future Continuous	*He will be having his washing machine fixed.*
Future Perfect Simple	*They will have had their roof repaired.*
be going to	*They're going to have the bedroom made bigger.*
modals (present)	*We must have the windows washed.*

The causative is formed in the following way:

have + object + past participle of the main verb

She had her wedding dress made.
They aren't having their flat decorated this year.
Has she had her eyes tested recently?

The object of the sentence must come directly before the past participle of the main verb.

We use the causative:

- to say that someone else has done something for us or on our behalf.
  David has mended his watch. (David did it himself.)
  David has had his watch mended. (Someone else did it for David.)

- to describe something unpleasant that has happened.
  They had their car stolen while they were away.
  Malcolm had his window broken.

Notes
When we are speaking, we can use the verb *get* instead of *have*.
He's getting his car repaired at the moment.

When we talk about unpleasant events, we cannot use *get* instead of *have*.

1
Write the words in the correct order.

Eg *her wedding dress / the bride / made / has had / by a top designer*

1 have had / they / by courier / sent / the invitations
   ....

2 his hair / has had / the groom / cut
   ....

3 done / is going to have / at home / she / her hair and make-up
   ....

4 to the church / the flowers / delivered / are having / they
   ....

5 all the food / are having / by a catering company / they / cooked
   ....

6 are having / by a professional photographer / they / taken / photographs
   ....

2
Complete the sentences with the Causative. Use the Present Simple or Present Continuous.

Eg We ...*have the house cleaned*... every Tuesday. (the house / clean)

1 She always .... by a top designer. (her clothes / make)

2 She .... so she'll have to wear her old one. (her new coat / clean)

3 My mother .... every six weeks. (her hair / do)

4 I .... for my birthday party. (a cake / make)

5 My daughter .... very often. (her eyes / not test)

6 We .... this afternoon because we're going out.
   (the new cooker / not deliver)

Complete the sentences with the Causative. Use the Past Simple or Past Continuous.

Eg We ...... *had the curtains cleaned* ...... last spring. (the curtains / clean)

1   He .... when I saw him. (his car / wash)
2   I .... last week. (my computer / fix)
3   He .... by the doctor. (his bandages / change)
4   We .... by the police officer. (our ID cards / check)
5   She .... when it started to rain. (her photo / take)
6   We .... yesterday so I missed my favourite programme.
    (the TV / repair)
7   I .... at the doctor's and it was normal. (my blood pressure / take)
8   We .... to the school last week. (the books / deliver)

Write sentences with the Causative.

Eg She *hasn't had her tooth taken out yet.*
    She's having it taken out tomorrow.
    (her tooth / take out)

1   She ....
    ....
    ....
    (her car / service)
2   I ....
    ....
    ....
    (the film / develop)
3   He ....
    ....
    ....
    (his boots / mend)

4   I ....
    ....
    ....
    (the X-rays / do)
5   He ....
    ....
    ....
    (his suit / dry-clean)
6   They ....
    ....
    ....
    (the damage / repair)

Complete the sentences with the Causative. Use the Past Perfect Simple.

Eg She ...... *had had all the reports photocopied* ...... by lunchtime. (all the reports / photocopy)

1   They .... for three years. (their flat / not paint)
2   They .... before the winter. (the roof / fix)
3   The baby .... soon after he was born. (his hearing / test)
4   He .... before starting the journey. (his tyres / check)
5   The tourists .... before they were allowed through the gates.
    (their bags / search)
6   He .... before he was fifty. (his books / not publish)
7   Her mother .... black. (her hair / dye)
8   Her brother's friend .... very short. (his hair / cut)

6 Complete the sentences with the Causative. Use the verbs from the box.

burgle	cut off	destroy	flood
break	spoil	steal	

Eg She *had her wallet stolen* . *(her wallet)*

1 They ....
.... because they
didn't pay the bill. (the electricity)

2 He ....
when he left the water running by mistake.
(his bathroom)

3 We ....
.... by a cricket ball.
(our sitting room window)

4 The museum ....
.... by the fire. (a valuable painting)

5 He ....
.... while he was
on holiday. (his house)

6 The Smith family ....
.... by other guests
in the restaurant smoking.
(their meal)

7 Write questions using the Causative.

Eg *they / their house / build / by the sea / ?*
Did they have their house built by the sea?

1 the twins / their photo / take / on Saturday / ?
....
....

2 Dad / his office / decorate / during the holidays / ?
....
....

3 he / flowers / send / to her / yesterday / ?
....
....

4 your brother / his leg / put / in plaster / ?
....

5 you / your old bike / repair / ?
....
....

6 the school / some new tennis courts / build / last
year / ?
....
....

8 Complete the questions using the Causative.

Eg *You see your friend with a different hairstyle.*
Have *you had your hair cut* *?* *(hair / cut)*

1 You meet someone you know at the optician's.
Are ....? (your eyes / test)

2 You see your father at the garage.
Are ....? (the car / wash)

3 You visit a friend whose house is now a different colour. (your house / paint)
When did ....?

4 You see a friend who is coming out of the dentist's holding her cheek.
Have ....? (a tooth / take out)

5 Your best friend suddenly appears wearing earrings.
Did .... yesterday? (your ears / pierce)

6 The radio at home isn't working properly.
When do you think you ....? (the radio / fix)

9 Complete the sentences with the words from the box.

cut   going   had (x2)   have (x2)   having   sent   were

Eg   *He is* ....*going*....................... *to have the car repaired tomorrow.*

1   I won't .... my car serviced tomorrow because I need it to go somewhere.
2   We .... our tickets changed so we were able to get a later flight.
3   We .... having our order taken when the fire alarm went off.
4   Will you please .... the flowers delivered to the following address?
5   My mother has her hair .... at the hairdresser's once every two months.
6   The group .... all its songs recorded at the same studio.
7   The company had all their documents .... by courier.
8   My boss is .... a special party organised for his retirement.

10 Write sentences using the Causative.

A   You have had your ideal home built.

Eg   *big house with two floors (build)*
     I've had a big house with two floors
     built.

1   swimming pool in the garden (put)
    ....
    ....

2   flowers and trees around the house (plant)
    ....
    ....

3   satellite dish on the roof (install)
    ....
    ....

B   You have had your car serviced.

1   the brakes (check)
    ....
    ....

2   the oil (change)
    ....
    ....

3   the engine (clean)
    ....
    ....

THINK
ABOUT IT!

Don't forget to put the past participle after the object of the sentence!

C   You have had a medical check-up done.

1   my blood pressure (take)
    ....
    ....

2   my blood (test)
    ....
    ....

3   my heart beat (measure)
    ....
    ....

11 Complete the sentences in your own words. Use the Causative.

Eg *During the last week, ...I have had my English composition marked by the teacher......*

1 Last Saturday morning, ...

2 Yesterday, ...

3 Next week, ...

4 Tomorrow, ...

5 Today, ...

6 Every month, ...

7 Once a year, ...

8 Next year, ...

Pairwork

Work with a partner. Pretend that you haven't seen each other for a year. Take turns to talk about things that you or your family have had done in the last year. For example:

We have had our house painted a different colour.
My dad has had his car fixed.

Writing

Write a letter to your penfriend in England, wishing them a happy summer. With the letter, you also send him a photo of your house and a photo of your family. Tell your penfriend what you and your family have had done recently and ask them about their family. Use the Causative as much as possible.

Dear ....,

....

....

....

....

....

....

....

....

Lots of love,

....

Clauses of Reason

We use clauses of reason to explain why something happens. They are introduced by a number of words and phrases.

as/since
because
the reason for + noun
the reason why + verb
because of + noun/the fact that
due to + noun/the fact that

As / Since I was late for the meeting, I took a taxi.
Mum made spaghetti because it's my favourite.
The reason for his bad behaviour was not clear.
The reason why he behaved badly was not clear.
Because of his bad health, he had to stop working.
Because of the fact that it had no batteries, the calculator wouldn't work.
Due to the traffic jam, I arrived late.
Due to the fact that she had a lot of work, they weren't able to go away on holiday.

Complete the sentences with the phrases from the box. Sometimes more than one is possible.

| as | because | because of | due to | since | the reason for | the reason why (x2) |

Eg ....*The reason for*.............. *their happiness was that their daughter had just had a baby girl!*

1 .... they preferred camping, they used to go to a camp-site every year for their holidays.

2 .... she left her job was that they made her work long hours.

3 She failed the exam .... the fact that she hadn't studied hard enough.

4 .... the bad weather, they didn't go out in the boat.

5 They decided to go to York for the weekend .... they had friends there.

6 .... she didn't come to the party was that she wasn't feeling very well.

7 On holiday, the children played lots of games .... they didn't have any schoolwork to do.

8 .... the fact that she had a job on the other side of town, she bought her own car.

Clauses of Purpose

We use clauses of purpose to explain why someone does something.
They are introduced by a number of words and phrases.

to + infinitive
in order to + infinitive
so that
in case
for

In order to + infinitive is more formal than *to* + infinitive. In negative sentences, we put the word *not* before the word *to*.
She went to Paris to study French.
She went to Paris in order to study French.
In order not to forget all her English over the holidays, she read lots of novels in English.

So that is followed by a verb in the Present Simple or *can/could* or *will/would*, depending on the meaning of the sentence.
Sarah saves her pocket money so that she can buy CDs with it.
I'm going to get up early tomorrow so that I will have plenty of time to get ready.

We never use *will* or *would* after *in case* even if we are talking about the future. In this case, we use the Present Simple or the Present Continuous.
Take some extra money in case you need it.

We use a gerund or a noun after the word *for*.
This knife is for cutting meat.
We went to a really nice fish restaurant for lunch.

Choose the correct answer.

Eg   They went for a walk (to) / so that *get some fresh air.*

1   I will take some sandwiches with me in case I *will get / get* hungry.
2   In order to *having / have* more time at the seaside, we left home early.
3   He uses his computer for *writing / write* all his letters.
4   Let's save up our money so that *to buy / we can buy* a new air-conditioning unit for the bedroom.
5   We'll take a bag with us in case we *catch / to catch* any fish.
6   They went into town in *order / case* to go to the post office.
7   I decided to take a boat to the island *to / for* see my grandmother.
8   Invite lots of people to the party *in case / in the case* some people can't come.

In case does not mean the same as if and you cannot use in case instead of if in conditional sentences.

Clauses of Contrast and Concession

We use clauses of contrast and concession to show some kind of 'disagreement' in a sentence. They are introduced by a number of words and phrases.

but
although/even though
in spite of/despite + noun/the fact that/-ing
however/nevertheless
while/whereas

We bought some jeans but we didn't find any trainers we liked.
Although/Even though the hotel wasn't near the sea, it was very nice.
Despite the heat, they had to cook meals every day for the tourists.
In spite of the fact that the exams were difficult, she thought that she had passed.
In spite of having a bad headache, she had to finish reading the book.
He eats a lot. However/Nevertheless, he isn't fat.
She loved dancing while he didn't like it at all.
This photo shows a castle whereas the other photo is of a fairground.
Whereas some pupils agreed with the teacher, others didn't.

Notes
We never put *of* after *despite.*
We always put a comma after *however.*

Complete the sentences with the words from the box. Sometimes more than one is possible.

| although | but | despite (x2) | even though | however | in spite | whereas | while |

Eg They wanted to make a cake. .... *However* ...., there were no eggs in the fridge.

1 .... the pain in his leg, he carried on running.

2 I enjoy horror films, ... my sister enjoys comedies.

3 We decided to go out for a walk .... it was raining.

4 I was very angry with Peter, ... I still invited him to my party.

5 .... of the fact that I said I was sorry, Mum is still angry with me.

6 .... most people enjoy going to the beach, I hate it.

7 I wanted to go out .... the others wanted to stay at home.

8 .... the heat, we went out for a walk.

Complete the sentences.

Eg The concert was very good. The singer wasn't famous.
Although *the singer wasn't famous, the concert was very good.* ....

1 He ran very fast but he still didn't win the race.
Despite ....

2 He likes meat and his wife likes vegetables.
Whereas he ....

3 They stayed up late talking. They felt very tired.
Even though ....

4 He was rich and famous but he wasn't happy.
In spite of ....

5 She already had three children. She wanted one more!
Although ....

Choose the correct answer.

Eg I want to know the reason .... he left.
  a for   b why   c as

1 Take a jumper .... it gets cold tonight.
  a so that   b due to   c in case

2 They went on a picnic .... the rain.
  a despite   b because of   c in spite

3 David likes football .... Alan likes tennis.
  a in spite of   b whereas   c however

4 Because of .... the match was cancelled.
  a raining   b to rain   c the rain

5 The reason .... the mistake is not clear.
  a why   b for   c so

6 .... she likes meat, she doesn't want roast beef.
  a Even   b In spite of   c Although

Clauses of Result

We use clauses of result to talk about the effects of an action. They are introduced by a number of words and phrases.

so
so+ adjective/adverb (that)
such + (a/an) adjective + noun (that)
as a result
therefore

We missed the bus, so we had to walk home.
The pizza was so hot that I couldn't eat it.
She plays the piano so well that she has already won lots of prizes.
It was such a nice day that we wanted to go for a picnic.
He failed some of his exams and, as a result, he had to take them again in September.
They lost their tickets for the concert. Therefore, they didn't see their favourite singer.

Notes
We also use:

- such a lot of + plural/uncountable noun.
  Molly has such a lot of toys in her bed that she can't lie down.
  There is such a lot of dust in here that I can't breathe!

- so much/little + uncountable noun.
  There is so much furniture in here that there isn't room to move!
  He knows so little English that he can't even say his name.

- so many/few + countable noun.
  I've seen so many films like this that I find them boring.
  She knows so few people that she's lonely.

6 Complete the sentences with **so, such** or **such a/an.**

Eg It was ....*such*................ a hot day that we spent all day in the sea.

1 There were .... a lot of people at the concert that we could hardly move.
2 They were .... happy when their first grandchild was born.
3 It was .... awful film that we left halfway through.
4 There were .... many people on the bus that we had to stand up all the way.
5 The little boy ran .... fast that I couldn't catch him.
6 He was .... good teacher that we all learnt a lot.
7 We saw .... many different kinds of video players that we didn't know which one to buy.
8 There were .... few people on the island in the winter that it seemed completely empty.

Rewrite the sentences using the words given. Use between two and five words.

Eg There were large crowds and we couldn't see the singers. **due**
    We couldn't see the singers ....*due to the*........... large crowds.

1 Although I put lots of sun cream on, I still got burnt. **spite**
   I still got burnt, ... lots of sun cream on.
2 My mother baked so many cakes that we were eating them for days! **such**
   My mother baked .... cakes that we were eating them for days!
3 Since he wanted to get good marks in the exams, he studied very hard. **order**
   He studied very hard .... good marks in the exams.
4 They thought the weather might get cool so they took jackets with them. **case**
   They took jackets with them .... cool.
5 They got to the restaurant early because they wanted to find a table next to the window. **that**
   They got to the restaurant early .... find a table next to the window.
6 She went to the party, despite feeling ill. **though**
   She went to the party, ... ill.
7 We left early because we were bored. **reason**
   The .... early was that we were bored.
8 We missed the train and so we had to walk home. **result**
   We missed the train and, ..., we had to walk home.

Find the extra word and write it in the space.

Eg They were such a nice people that we invited them to lunch the next day. ....*a*..........

1 The reason why for the children were happy was that they were on holiday! ....
2 They got up early, despite of the fact that they hadn't had much sleep. ....
3 There were so such many children at the party that they made a lot of noise. ....
4 There weren't enough chairs, so that we got some from another table. ....
5 He left his job because due of his illness. ....
6 He turned on the television for to listen to the news. ....
7 In spite of he spending all day working, he still had to take work home. ....
8 We went on a holiday to Greece because of we were interested in the historical sites. ....

Match.

Eg Since the children were very tired,   a However, she was always hungry again by lunchtime.
1   She had a good breakfast every morning.   b they went to bed early.
2   In order to have some peace and quiet,   c so that Dad could talk on the phone.
3   He liked golf   d whereas his friend preferred tennis.
4   We turned the radio down   e he was still able to concentrate on his work.
5   It was such a bad meal   f that we complained.
6   You should wear trainers   g they couldn't wait to go on holiday.
7   Despite all the noise   h she went to her room and locked the door.
8   Although they enjoyed school,   i in case you have to walk a long way.

Complete the text by writing one word in each gap.

A Visit to the Zoo

Last Saturday, Jim and Tonic didn't have a lot of jobs to do (Eg) ....*so*............. they

decided to go to the zoo. The zoo is Tonic's favourite place (1) .... he knows

so (2) .... of the animals and birds there. Jim took his camera in

(3) .... there were any new animals.

The first place they went to in the zoo was the monkey house. The monkeys all made so

(4) .... noise that Jim and Tonic couldn't hear themselves speak! They

laughed a lot (5) .... of all the funny things the monkeys did, though.

Next, they went to the elephant house (6) .... they didn't stay there long

(7) .... to the terrible smell! They quickly went outside (8) ....

have a look at the baby elephant with

its mother. Then they had to hurry in

order (9) .... to miss

feeding-time for the seals, which were

very good at catching the fish the keepers

threw to them! After seeing a few more

animals and lots of colourful birds, it was

time to go home.

(10) .... though

Tonic was tired, he didn't want to go

home. (11) ...., Jim

said, 'Come on, Tonic, it's been such a

nice day (12) I

think I've had enough now. I'll buy you

an ice cream before we go home.'

Tonic thought that was a good idea.

Complete the sentences in your own words.

Eg   I am so ....*happy that I could sing!*....................................

1   The reason for going to school ....

2   I like learning English because ....

3   I got up early last week in order to ....

4   I always carry .... in my bag, in case ....

5   The reason why I like ....

6   Due to the cold/hot weather I ....

7   I should eat lots of fresh fruit so that ....

8   Although I live in ....

Work with a partner. Plan the main ideas of a descriptive story together. Decide what you are going to describe – a visit to an interesting place, a special holiday, etc – and talk about what you think your story should be like.

 **Writing**

Using your ideas from Pairwork above, write a short story. Use as many phrases from the unit as you can. Use your imagination to make the story more interesting.

Last year, ...
....
....
....
....

Although, ...
....
....
....
....
....

Despite ....
....
....
....
....
....

In the end, ...
....
....
....
....

1 Match.

Eg Skyscrapers are buildings ——————— a which are extremely tall.

1 Mobile phones are phones   b that contain a huge amount of information.

2 Dustmen are people   c that you can carry with you.

3 Noel Gallagher is a musician   d where you can see lots of beautiful architecture.

4 Rome is the place   e who collect all our rubbish.

5 Encyclopedias are books   f who sing in rock groups?

6 Do you know many people   g who is a member of the group Oasis.

2 Choose the correct answer.

Eg Are you the person .... looks after the snakes and lizards at the zoo?
     a what   b whose   c who

1 Did you see the film .... was on television at eleven o'clock last night?
     a which   b what   c where

2 I don't know the chef .... son is in my class.
     a who   b whose   c which

3 I once went to a small village .... they only eat fish.
     a which   b where   c when

4 My friend Denise is the person .... clothes I borrow.
     a who   b which   c whose

5 Where's the person .... sold you this car?
     a whose   b -   c who

6 Have you found the book .... you lost yesterday?
     a that   b what   c where

7 I've never met the woman .... owns that new shoe shop.
     a who   b whose   c who's

8 Leo's the person .... I have invited to my house on Saturday.
     a -   b which   c whose

3 Find the mistakes and write the sentences correctly.

Eg My parents, which live in central London, would love to live in the country.
My parents, who live in central London, would love to live in the country.

1 Where's the pair of jeans what you were wearing yesterday?

....

....

2 My aunt and uncle who live in America, are coming to stay with us.

....

....

3 My favourite car, is a Mercedes, is too expensive for me to buy.

....

....

4 Have you been to the new clothes shop where is next to the bank?

....

....

5 Shakespeare is a writer which plays I enjoy watching on stage.

....

....

6 The Acropolis which is a popular tourist attraction is in Athens.

....

....

7 Mel Gibson, is an actor, has got lovely eyes.

....

....

8 Do you know a man can fix my car?

....

....

4 Choose the correct answer.

Eg   I can't help .... so clever!
   a to be   **b** it being   **c** being

1   Jim loves .... in the winter.
   a skiing   **b** the skiing   **c** to skiing

2   I forgot .... the plants this morning.
   a watered   **b** watering   **c** to water

3   I imagine .... on the moon would be
   extremely strange!
   a to live   **b** being lived   **c** living

4   Do you mind .... me your laptop for the
   weekend?
   a lending   **b** to lend   **c** to lending

5   I can't persuade Mum .... me come to the
   party this evening.
   a to let   **b** let   **c** letting

6   Janet never goes anywhere without .... her
   make-up.
   a she puts on   **b** putting on   **c** to put on

7   I hate .... you, but can you give me some
   more money?
   a be asking   **b** asking   **c** to asking

8   .... is an excellent form of exercise.
   a To swim   **b** The swimming   **c** Swimming

5 Complete the sentences with Gerunds or
Infinitives.

Eg   We planned ....to go........ to the coast at the
   weekend, but the weather wasn't good. (go)

1   He admitted .... about where he'd
   got the money. (lie)

2   Where did you learn .... so well?
   (drive)

3   If you can't get a good picture on the TV, try
   .... the side of it with your hand. (hit)

4   Don't forget .... the dog before
   you go out this evening. (feed)

5   Did you finish .... your room
   yesterday? (decorate)

6   He isn't very good at .... a computer.
   (use)

7   I'm so happy .... you again after so
   long! (see)

8   It was a long journey so we stopped ....
   something to eat on the way. (get)

6 Find the mistakes and write the sentences correctly.

Eg   We're really looking forward to see you at Christmas!
   We're really looking forward to seeing you at Christmas!
   ....

1   Did you manage find your purse?
   ....

2   I hope seeing you during the weekend.
   ....

3   It's just too hot for going out today.
   ....

4   In the summer she usually goes to windsurf.
   ....

5   Is the coffee enough cool to drink yet?
   ....

6   Do you regret to drive your car while you were tired?
   ....

7   Do you remember to meet those Dutch people last year?
   ....

8   I often spend time to surf the Internet.
   ....

7 Complete the sentences with the Causative. Use the verbs from the box.

clean   decorate   dye   make   not cut
not pay   search   service   test

Eg   I *haven't had my hair cut* for ages. (hair)

1   At the border between the two countries, everyone .... (their cars)

2   He .... at the garage when I saw him. (car)

3   She .... for her wedding next year. (a special dress)

4   I .... once a year. (my eyes)

5   They .... into their bank. (their salary)

6   We .... this summer. (our house)

7   An athlete I saw on TV .... green! (his hair)

8   We .... in the spring. (our carpets)

8 Complete the sentences by writing one word in each gap.

Eg   Are they going to ....*have*........ the car washed before they go away?

1   My sister .... her hair dyed a different colour every year.

2   The company .... having all its advertising done quite cheaply this year.

3   I .... going to have my hair done tomorrow.

4   My father was .... a reception organised for some visiting businessmen.

5   My brother has .... the walls of his room painted blue.

6   She had all her jewellery .... in the burglary.

7   Luckily, we had .... our TV repaired by the time the World Cup started.

8   He .... having all the wine delivered to his shop tomorrow.

9 Write questions using the Causative. Use the Past Simple.

Eg   you / your arm / bandage / at the hospital / ?
Did you have your arm bandaged at the hospital?
....

1   she / the new cooker / deliver / yesterday / ?
....

2   you / your old sewing machine / mend / last month / ?
....

3   the college / a new gym / build / last year / ?
....

4   they / their party / organise / by Phil / ?
....

5   the couple / their photo / take / outside the church / ?
....

6   your grandmother / her flat / paint / last week / ?
....

7   she / the books / send / to her / from England / ?
....

8   he / his beard / shave off / before Easter / ?
....

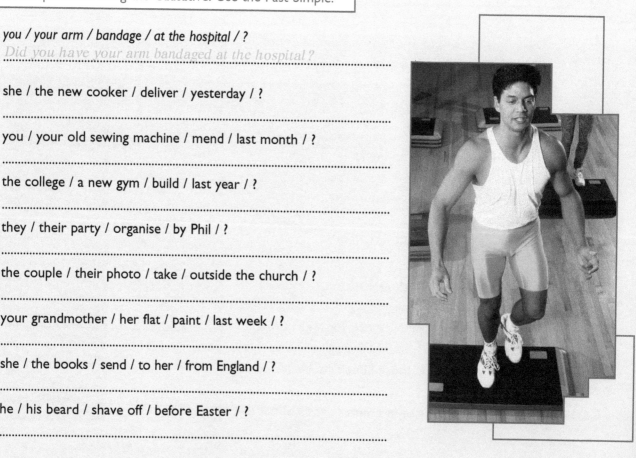

Complete the sentences with the phrases from the box. Sometimes more than one is possible.

| as | because | because of | due to | in case | in order to | since | so that | the reason why | to |

Eg They saved up their money ....*so that*............... they could have a nice summer holiday every year.

1 .... they had three children, they decided to move to a bigger house.
2 .... his bad health, he couldn't travel.
3 .... they wanted to go to Tenerife was that some friends had recommended it.
4 He went to the shops .... buy some food for the weekend.
5 .... keep fit, she went to aerobics classes three times a week.
6 My friends didn't come to the party .... they had visitors.
7 Take some games with you .... the children get bored on the journey.
8 .... the extreme heat, we put on the air-conditioning.

Complete the sentences with the words from the box. Sometimes more than one is possible.

| although | but | in spite of | even though | however | so (x2) | such a/an | whereas |

Eg ....*Whereas*............... I prefer holidays by the sea, my husband prefers mountain holidays.

1 .... she was feeling ill, she still went to work.
2 A lot of children wanted to go on the school trip .... the school booked three coaches.
3 It was .... hot day that all we wanted to do was to swim in the sea.
4 She worked hard all day and came home late. ...., she still went out in the evening with her friends.
5 The professor spoke .... quickly that I couldn't understand him.
6 My husband liked the coffee-coloured curtains, ... I bought the pink ones!
7 .... we arrived at the airport at the correct time, we had to wait five hours before we left.
8 .... not working very hard, she managed to pass all her exams!

Choose the correct answer.

Eg I had never seen .... wonderful view before.
   a so   b such   c such a

1 I didn't know that there were .... churches in this city!
   a such a lot   b so many   c so much

2 In spite of .... a bad headache, she still managed to organise the children's party.
   a to have   b having   c she had

3 The journey was difficult because of the rain. ...., we got there safely in the end.
   a Although   b Whereas   c However

4 Where did you find .... lovely garden furniture?
   a such a   b so   c such

5 They didn't pay the bill and, ..., they had the electricity cut off.
   a as a result   b the reason   c even though

6 It was Pete's birthday .... he decided to take some friends to the cinema.
   a so that   b while   c so

7 .... his bad behaviour, the headmaster had to have a word with him.
   a Since   b Because of   c Due

8 We should fill up with petrol now, in case we .... another petrol station on the way.
   a don't find   b find   c won't find

Irregular verbs

Infinitive	Past Simple	Past Participle	Infinitive	Past Simple	Past Participle
be	was/were	been	lend	lent	lent
beat	beat	beaten	let	let	let
become	became	become	lie	lay	lain
begin	began	begun	light	lit	lit
bite	bit	bitten	lose	lost	lost
blow	blew	blown	make	made	made
break	broke	broken	mean	meant	meant
bring	brought	brought	meet	met	met
build	built	built	pay	paid	paid
burst	burst	burst	put	put	put
buy	bought	bought	read	read	read
catch	caught	caught	ride	rode	ridden
choose	chose	chosen	ring	rang	rung
come	came	come	rise	rose	risen
cost	cost	cost	run	ran	run
cut	cut	cut	say	said	said
deal	dealt	dealt	see	saw	seen
dig	dug	dug	sell	sold	sold
do	did	done	send	sent	sent
draw	drew	drawn	shake	shook	shaken
drink	drank	drunk	shine	shone	shone
drive	drove	driven	shoot	shot	shot
eat	ate	eaten	show	showed	shown
fall	fell	fallen	shut	shut	shut
feed	fed	fed	sing	sang	sung
feel	felt	felt	sit	sat	sat
fight	fought	fought	sleep	slept	slept
find	found	found	speak	spoke	spoken
fly	flew	flown	spend	spent	spent
forbid	forbade	forbidden	spill	spilt	spilt
forget	forgot	forgotten	spread	spread	spread
forgive	forgave	forgiven	spring	sprang	sprung
freeze	froze	frozen	stand	stood	stood
get	got	got	steal	stole	stolen
give	gave	given	stick	stuck	stuck
go	went	gone	sting	stung	stung
grow	grew	grown	sweep	swept	swept
have	had	had	swim	swam	swum
hear	heard	heard	take	took	taken
hide	hid	hidden	teach	taught	taught
hit	hit	hit	tell	told	told
hold	held	held	think	thought	thought
hurt	hurt	hurt	throw	threw	thrown
keep	kept	kept	understand	understood	understood
know	knew	known	wake	woke	woken
lay	laid	laid	wear	wore	worn
lead	led	led	win	won	won
leave	left	left	write	wrote	written